Beginning Microsoft Word 2010

Career Step, LLC
Phone: 801.489.9393
Toll-Free: 800.246.7837
Fax: 801.491.6645
careerstep.com

This text companion contains a snapshot of the online program content converted to a printed format. Please note that the online training program is constantly changing and improving and is always the source of the most up-to-date information.

Product Number: HG-PR-11-114
Generation Date: January 16, 2013

© Career Step - All Rights Reserved.
The material in this book may not be copied or distributed without express written consent from Career Step.

Table of Contents

Unit 1
Introduction

Introduction to Beginning Microsoft Word 2010

Learning Objectives

Microsoft Word Fundamentals – Students will be able to create, save, open, and edit a document.

Working with Text – Students will be able to edit and format text with options such as alignment, fonts, lists, margins, spacing, tab stops, page format, and layout.

Search and Review Tools – Students will be able to employ the available search and review tools, including spell and grammar check, autocorrect, find and replace, search, format painter, copy, paste, the clipboard, and document view options.

Working with Tables – Students will be able to create, format, edit, and sort tables.

Themes and Styles – Students will be able to apply, modify, and delete document themes and styles.

Microsoft Word is a powerful word-processing program that gives users the tools to create a variety of professional documents. Word automatically checks your spelling and grammar and corrects common mistakes. It even lets you insert charts, tables, and pictures into your documents. Microsoft Word is the most widely used and, according to most reviews, the most powerful and user-friendly word-processor available. This module will teach you how to format pages, work with themes, styles, and pictures, create and format tables, and much more.

This training contains specific references to the 2010 version of Microsoft Office for Windows. While most concepts and procedures outlined are consistent across versions of Microsoft Office, each version is slightly different. If you are using an older version of Microsoft Office, you may need to download and run a compatibility package to use files created with newer versions. Compatibility information and updates can be found at Microsoft.com. If you are completing this training on a Mac, remember that Mac versions of Microsoft Office differ significantly from Windows versions in functionality, interface, and workflows.

Before beginning this module, it's important for you to know that you do not need Microsoft Office software to complete this training. Any practice files included as part of this training are for your personal educational benefit only. If you want to download a 60-day trial version of Microsoft Office, you can visit office.microsoft.com/en-us/try/. For Mac users, visit www.microsoft.com/mac/trial.

Unit 2
Microsoft Word Fundamentals

Microsoft Word Fundamentals – Introduction

This unit will teach you the basics of Microsoft Word. You'll learn about the main parts of the program screen, how to give commands, use help, and about new features in Word 2010.

Let's get started!

Starting Word

In order to use a program, you must start—or launch—it first.

If you are upgrading to a new Windows platform, you will find both similarities and differences between the newest versions and the older version of Windows you have worked on previously.

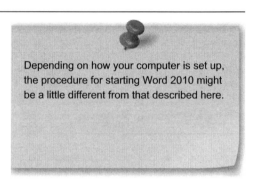

Depending on how your computer is set up, the procedure for starting Word 2010 might be a little different from that described here.

If you use Word 2010 frequently, you might consider pinning it to the Start menu. To do this, right-click Microsoft Word 2010 in the All Programs menu and select Pin to Start Menu from the contextual menu. Windows 7 users can also pin a program to the taskbar. To do this, right-click the Word button in the taskbar and select Pin this program to taskbar from the contextual menu.

Windows Vista and Windows 7

1. Click the Start button. The Start menu will appear.
2. Click All Programs. The left pane of the Start menu will display the programs and menus installed on your computer.
3. Click Microsoft Office.
4. Select Microsoft Office Word 2010. The Word 2010 program screen will appear.

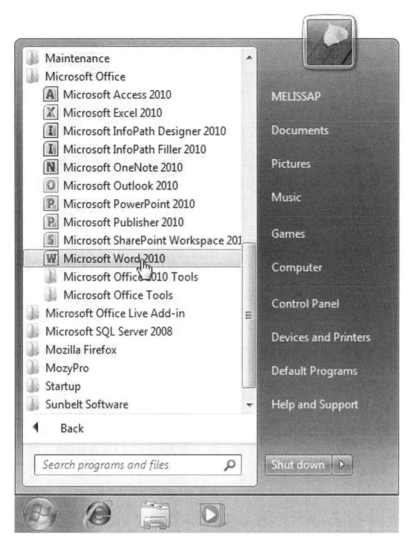

Understanding the Word 2010 Program Screen

The Word 2010 program screen may seem confusing and overwhelming at first. This lesson will help you become familiar with the Word 2010 program screen as well as the new user interface.

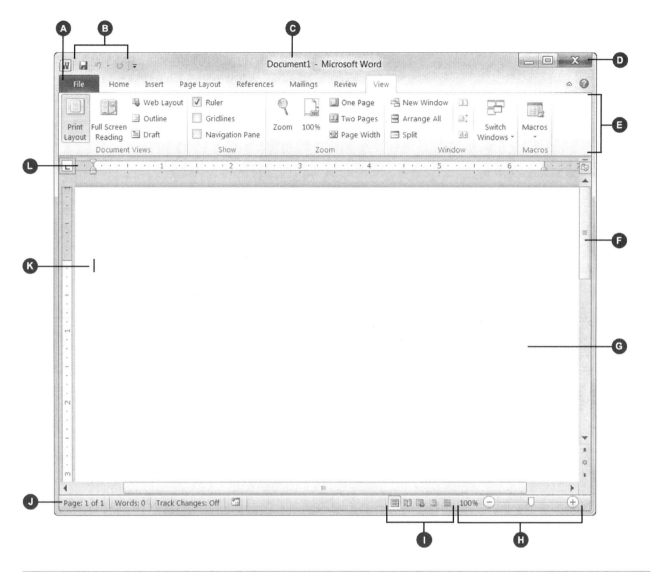

A	**File tab:** Contains basic file management commands—such as New, Open, Save, and Close—and program options.
B	**Quick Access Toolbar:** Contains common commands such as Save and Undo. You can add more commands as well.
C	**Title bar:** Displays the name of the program you are using and the name of the document you are currently working on.
D	**Close button:** Click here to close the current document. If only one document is open, clicking this button will close the Word program also.
E	**Ribbon:** The tabs on the Ribbon replace the menus and toolbars found in previous versions of Word.
F	**Scroll bars:** There are both vertical and horizontal scroll bars: you use them to view and move in your document.
G	**Document window:** This is where you enter and work on document content.
H	**Zoom slider:** Click and drag the slider to zoom in or out of a slide. You can also use the + and – buttons.

I	**View shortcuts:** Quickly switch between Print Layout, Full Screen Reading, Web Layout, Outline, and Draft views.
J	**Status bar:** Displays information about your document. Right-click it to specify which information is shown.
K	**Insertion Point:** The small, blinking bar controls where document content is entered. Move the insertion point with the mouse, or the arrow keys on the keyboard.
L	**Ruler:** Displays left and right paragraph indents, document margins, and tab stops. Click the View Ruler button above the vertical scroll bar to view or hide the ruler.

I. MATCHING.
Match the correct term to the definition.

1. _B_ displays information about your document

2. _G_ closes the current document

3. _E_ where you enter and work on document content

4. _H_ its tabs replace the menus and toolbars found in previous versions of Word

5. _D_ displays left and right paragraph indents, document margins, and tab stops

6. _C_ the blinking bar that controls where document content is entered

7. _A_ contains basic file management commands

8. _F_ displays the name of the program you are using and document you are currently working on

A. File tab
B. status bar
C. insertion point
D. ruler
E. document window
F. title bar
G. Close button
H. Ribbon

Giving Commands in Word – Lesson 1

Word 2010 provides easy access to commands through the Ribbon, File tab, and Quick Access Toolbar.

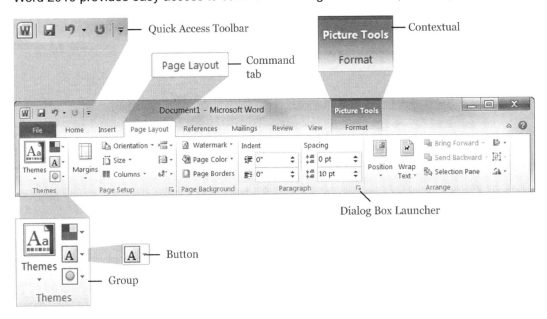

Ribbon

The Ribbon keeps commands visible while you work instead of hiding them under menus or toolbars, and it is the primary way to give commands in Word 2010.

You can hide the Ribbon so that only tab names appear, giving you more room in the program window. To do this, double-click the currently displayed command tab. Or, right-click a Ribbon tab and select Minimize Ribbon from the contextual menu. To display the Ribbon again, click any tab. Or, click the Minimize the Ribbon button.

The Ribbon is made up of three basic components: tabs, groups, and buttons.

Tabs: Commands are organized into tabs on the Ribbon. Each tab contains a different set of commands. There are three different types of tabs:

Command tabs: These tabs appear by default whenever you open the Word 2010 program. In Word 2010, the Home, Insert, Page Layout, References, Mailings, Review, and View tabs appear by default.

Contextual tabs: Contextual tabs appear whenever you perform a specific task and offer commands relative to only that task. For example, whenever you select a picture, the Format tab appears in the Ribbon under Picture Tools.

Program tabs: If you switch to a different authoring mode or view, such as Print Preview, program tabs replace the default command tabs that appear on the Ribbon.

Groups: The commands found on each tab are organized into groups of related commands. For example, the Font group contains commands used for formatting fonts. Click the Dialog Box Launcher (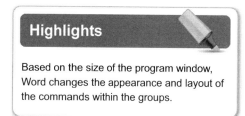) in the bottom-right corner of a group to display even more commands. The Dialog Box Launcher is a very important button in a group. Many of the familiar dialog boxes from previous versions of Word can be found here. For example, click the Dialog Box Launcher in the Font group to open the Font dialog box. Here, more options are available than those in the Font group on the Ribbon.

Highlights

Based on the size of the program window, Word changes the appearance and layout of the commands within the groups.

It is important to understand that groups change depending on how wide the Ribbon is. If the Ribbon does not fully extend across the screen or a low screen resolution is used, there will not be enough room to display all the commands on the Ribbon. Instead, the options will be grouped under one button.

The Ribbon with the groups hidden so only the tab names appear.

Buttons: One way to issue a command is by clicking its button on the Ribbon. Buttons are the smallest element of the Ribbon and change color when clicked.

9

Giving Commands in Word – Lesson 2

Near the Ribbon at the top of the program window are two other tools you can use to give commands in Word 2010: the File tab and the Quick Access Toolbar.

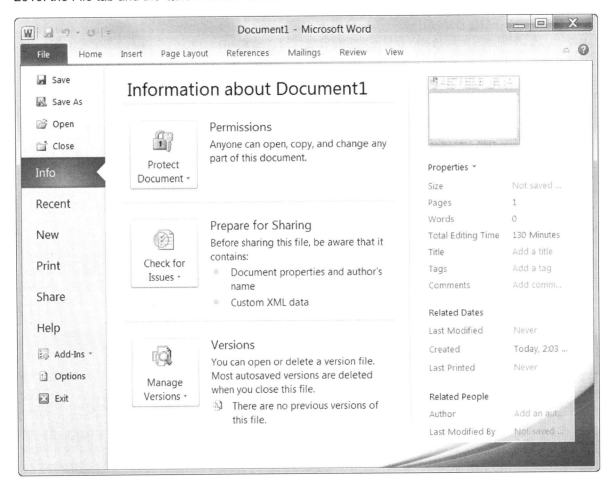

The Info tab in Backstage view.

File tab

In Word 2010, the File tab replaces the File menu and Office Button found in previous versions of Word.

The File tab appears in the upper-left corner of the program window. When clicked, it opens Backstage view, which is where you find commands for basic file management, including New, which creates a new file; Open, which opens an existing file; Save, which saves the currently opened file; and Close, which closes the currently opened file. This is also where you find commands for controlling program options and sharing.

Quick Access Toolbar

The Quick Access Toolbar appears to the right of the File tab and provides easy access to the commands you use most frequently. By default, the Save, Undo, and Redo buttons appear on the toolbar; however, you can customize this toolbar to meet your needs by adding or removing buttons.

I. **TRUE/FALSE.**
   Mark the following true or false.

1. The Quick Access Toolbar replaces the File menu and Office Button found in previous versions of Word.

   ○ true
   ◉ false

2. Buttons are the smallest element of the Ribbon and change color when clicked.

   ◉ true
   ○ false

3. The Ribbon contains basic commands, similar to the menus and toolbars of previous versions.

   ◉ true
   ○ false

Using Command Shortcuts – Lesson 1

Command shortcuts provide other ways to give commands in Word. Shortcuts can be a time-saving and efficient alternative to the Ribbon. Use shortcuts for the commands you use most frequently. For example, copying and pasting items between documents is much faster using keystroke shortcuts than it is using buttons on the Ribbon.

Keystroke Shortcuts

Keystroke shortcuts are one of the fastest ways to give commands in Word 2010. They're especially great for issuing common commands, such as saving a document or undoing your last action.

In order to issue a command using a keystroke shortcut, you simply press a combination of keys on your keyboard. For example, rather than clicking the Copy button on the Ribbon to copy text, you could press and hold the copy keystroke shortcut, CTRL + C. Or to practice opening a new document window, press CTRL + N.

Keystroke shortcuts are efficient because they allow both hands to work together. The right hand can run the mouse while the left issues the commands on the keyboard.

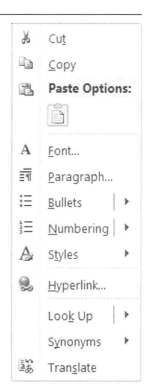

Common Keystroke Shortcuts	
CTRL + O	Opens a new document.
CTRL + N	Creates a new document.
CTRL + S	Saves the current document.
CTRL + P	Prints the document.
CTRL + B	Toggles bold font formatting.

CTRL + I	Toggles italic font formatting.
CTRL + C	Copies the selected text or object.
CTRL + X	Cuts the selected text or object.
CTRL + V	Pastes the selected text or object.
CTRL + Home	Moves the insertion point to the beginning of the document.
CTRL + End	Moves the insertion point to the end of the document.

There are two tools that you can use in Word 2010 that make relevant commands even more readily available: contextual menus and the Mini Toolbar.

Contextual menus

A contextual menu displays a list of commands related to a specific object or area. If you would like to practice using a contextual menu, try these steps:

1. Right-click an object or area of the document or program screen. A contextual menu appears, displaying commands that are relevant to the object or area that you right-clicked.
2. Select an option from the contextual menu, or click anywhere outside the contextual menu to close it without selecting anything.

Using Command Shortcuts – Lesson 2

Mini Toolbar

The Mini Toolbar will appear whenever you select text and contains common text formatting commands. To view the Mini Toolbar:

1. Select a block of text. The Mini Toolbar will appear near the text you selected. Sometimes the Mini Toolbar can be hard to see due to its transparency. To make the Mini Toolbar more visible, point to it.
2. Click a button on the Mini Toolbar. The command is given in Word.

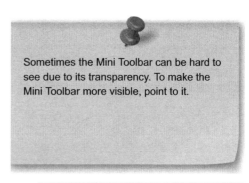

Sometimes the Mini Toolbar can be hard to see due to its transparency. To make the Mini Toolbar more visible, point to it.

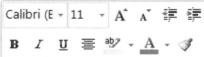

Highlights

If you don't want the Mini Toolbar to appear every time you select a block of text, click the File tab and click Options. Click the Personalize category, uncheck the Show Mini Toolbar on selection check box, and click OK.

Key Tips

Key Tips appear whenever you press the ALT key. You can use Key Tips to perform just about any action in Word 2010, without ever having to use the mouse.

Key Tips are a great way to issue commands by keyboard if you aren't sure of the keystroke shortcut. To issue a command using a Key Tip, first press the ALT key. Tiny letters and numbers, called badges, appear on the Office Button, the Quick Access Toolbar, and all of the tabs on the Ribbon. Depending on the command you want to issue, press the letter or number key indicated on the badge. Repeat this step as necessary until the desired command has been issued.

Key Tip badge

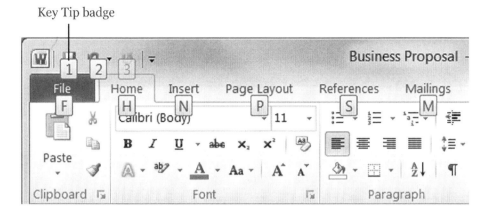

I. **TRUE/FALSE.**
Mark the following true or false.

1. You need to use the mouse when performing tasks with Key Tips.
   ◯ true
   ⦿ false

2. Keystroke shortcuts allow you to use both hands—one for the mouse and one for keyboard commands.
   ⦿ true
   ◯ false

3. When you press the ALT key, badges appear on all the tabs on the Ribbon.
   ⦿ true
   ◯ false

Creating a New Document

Creating a new document is one of the most basic commands you need in Word. A new document will appear automatically upon starting Word, but it's also helpful to know how to create a new document within the application. You can create a new blank document, such as the one that will appear when you open Word, or you can create a new document based on a template.

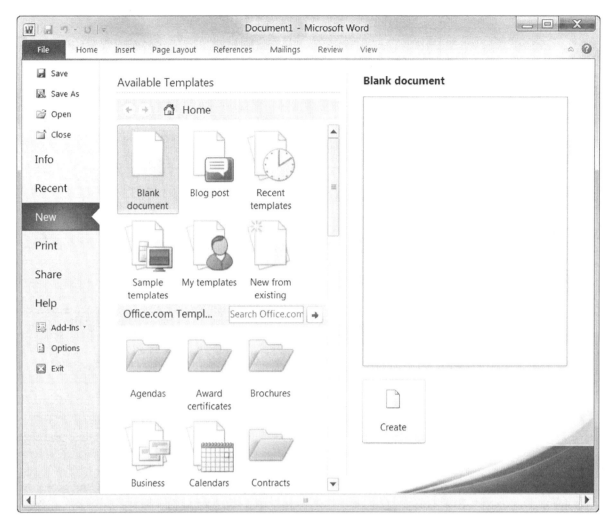

The New tab of Backstage view.

Create a new blank document

1. Click the File tab on the Ribbon and select **New**. The New tab of Backstage view will appear. By default, the Blank Document option is already selected.

2. Make sure the Blank document option is selected and click Create. The new blank document will appear in the Word application screen.

Other ways to create a blank document are to double-click the Blank Document option or to press CTRL + N.

Create a document from a template

A template is a combination of coordinated colors, layouts, and font styles for those who either don't have the time or don't feel like they have an eye for design.

1. Click the File tab and select New. The New Document dialog box will appear. There are several ways you can create a new document from a template. Different categories are listed below:

   Recent templates: Select a template in the Recently Used Templates area and click Create.

   Blog Post: If you have a Web log (or blog), you can create a blog entry using Word's blog template and post the entry directly to your blog.

Sample templates: Click this category to view templates that are already installed on your computer. Select a template and click Create.

My templates: Select My Templates to open a dialog box that displays templates you have created and saved on your computer.

New from existing: Select New from Existing to open a dialog box that allows you to browse for a document on your computer that you want to base a new document on. This is essentially like creating a copy of an existing file.

Office.com Templates: Click a category to view templates that you can download from Office Online. Find the template you want to use and click Download.

I. **MULTIPLE CHOICE.**
   Choose the best answer.

   1. Which of the following is not a way to create a new blank document?
      ○ Click the File tab on the Ribbon and select New.
      ○ Press CTRL + N.
      ◉ Right-click and select New Document.
      ○ Double-click the Blank Document option.

   2. Which template category do these instructions fall under: Click a category to view templates, find the one you want, and click Download?
      ○ My templates
      ○ Blank and recent
      ○ Installed templates
      ◉ Office.com Templates

   3. Which of the following is a true statement concerning creating a new document?
      ○ Select My Templates to browse for a document that you want to base a new document on.
      ◉ A new document will automatically appear when you open Word.
      ○ There is only one way to create a new document from a template.
      ○ none of the above

Opening a Document

Opening a document lets you work on a document that you or someone else has previously created and then saved. This lesson explains how to open a saved document.

You can locate a document on your computer and simply double-click it to open it, but you can also open a document from within the Word program.

1. Click the File tab and select Open. The Open dialog box will appear. You can also press CTRL + O to open a new document. Next, you will need to tell Word where the file you want to open is located.

2. Navigate to the location of the saved file. The Open dialog box has several controls that make it easy to navigate to locations and find files on your computer:

   Address bar: Click a link in the Address bar to open it. Click the arrow to the right of a link to open a list of folder within that location. Select a folder from the list to open it.

   Folders List: Shortcuts to common locations on your computer, such as the Desktop and Documents Folder.

   Search box: This searches the contents—including subfolders—of that window for the text that you type. If a file's name, file content, tags, or other file properties match the searched text, it will appear in the search results. Search results appear as you enter text in the search box.

To open a document that has been used recently, click the File tab, click Recent, and select a document from the Recent Documents list.

Highlights

You can pin a document to the Recent Documents list so that it is always available there. Click the Pin this document to the Recent Documents list button next to the document that you want to always be available. Click it again to remove the document from the Recent Documents list.

Folders List   Address Bar   Search Box

3. Select the file you want to open and click Open. Word will display the file in the application window.

Previewing and Printing a Document

Once you have created a document, and your computer is connected to a printer, you can print a copy. Before you do this, it's a good idea to preview how it's going to look. One thing of note is that the Print command automatically provides a preview of the document.

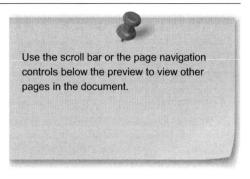

Use the scroll bar or the page navigation controls below the preview to view other pages in the document.

1. Click the File tab and select Print. Notice that the print settings and a preview of the document appear together, with print settings on the left and a preview on the right. After previewing the document, you can specify printing options, such as which pages or the number of copies to print.

2. Specify printing options and click the Print button. The document is sent to the printer. Another way to preview and print is to press CTRL + P.

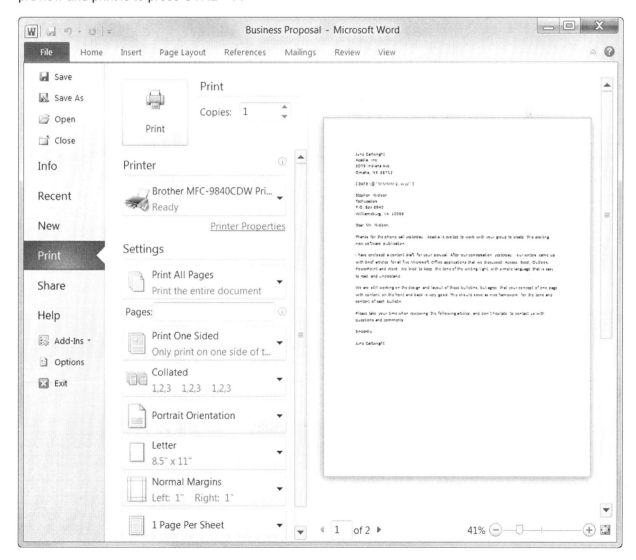

The Print Settings and Print Preview as shown in Backstage view. Use the print settings in the left column to control how the document is printed. Use the print preview area in the right column to preview how the document will look when printed.

Saving a Document – Lesson 1

After you've created a document, you need to save it if you want to use it again. Also, if you make changes to a document you'll want to save it. You can even save a copy of an existing document by using a different file type or by renaming it and saving it to a different location.

By default, all documents created in Word 2010 are saved using the new Word XML format (.docx). There are several benefits of these new formats for developers and individuals:

Compact files: Files are automatically compressed (or zipped) and can be up to 75% smaller. This reduces disk space required to store files and bandwidth required to send files.

Improved file recovery: Damaged or corrupted files are easier to recover.

Better privacy and control over personal information: Documents can be shared confidentially because sensitive information can easily be removed using the Document Inspector.

Better integration and interoperability of business data: Using XML as the framework for files means anyone can use and license the files, royalty free. All you need to open and edit an Office file is a ZIP utility and an XML editor.

Easier detection of documents that contain macros: Files that are saved in the default "x" suffix (.docx) cannot contain macros. Only files with the "m" suffix (.docm) can contain macros.

If you open a document that was created in an earlier version of Word in Word 2010, a dialog box will appear at some point asking if you would like to convert (save) the file to 2010 format. For more information about when you would/would not want to do this, see the Converting Documents lesson in the Collaborating with Other Programs chapter.

Save a new document

1. Click the Save button on the Quick Access Toolbar. The Save As dialog box will appear. Another way to save is press CTRL + S. Or, click the File tab and select Save.

2. Specify the drive and/or folder where you want to save your document. The Save As dialog box has several controls that make it easy to navigate to locations on your computer:

   Address bar: Click a link in the Address bar to open it. Click the arrow to the right of a link to open a list of folders within that location. Select a folder from the list to open it.

   Favorite Links: Shortcuts to common locations on your computer, such as the Desktop and Documents Folder.

   Folders List: View the hierarchy of drives and folders on your computer by expanding the Folders list.

3. Enter the file name in the File name text box.

4. Click Save.

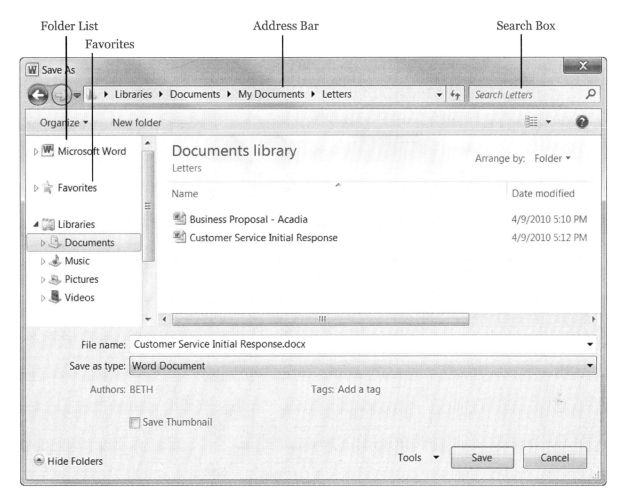

Folder List   Favorites   Address Bar   Search Box

If you open a document that was created in an earlier version of Word in Word 2010, a dialog box will appear at some point asking if you would like to convert (save) the file to 2010 format.

Save document changes

To save document changes, simply click the Save button on the Quick Access Toolbar. Any changes you have made to the document will be saved. Another way to save is to Press CTRL + S. Or simply click the File tab and select Save.

Saving a Document – Lesson 2

Save a document under a different name and/or location

Saving a document under a different name or in a different location does not delete the original file. It saves a copy of the file under a new name or in a new location.

1. Click the File tab and select Save As. The Save As dialog box will appear.

2. Enter a different name for the file in the File name text box. Navigate to a new location to save the file as necessary.

3. Click Save.

Save a document as a different file type

Just as some people can speak several languages, Word can read and write in other file formats. Saving a document in a different file type makes it easier to share information between programs. For example, you may want to save a document as a .pdf so that others can view it.

1. Click the File tab and select Save As. A Save As dialog box will appear.

2. Click the Save as type list arrow and select a file format. The table below provides brief descriptions of some of the file formats you can use to save a document.

3. Click Save. A copy of the document is saved in the new format.

Common Word File Formats	
Word Document (.docx)	This is the default format for Word 2010 documents.
Word Macro-Enabled Document (.docm)	This file format supports macros in Word 2010.
Word 97-2003 Document (.doc)	Documents in this format can be read/used by all versions of Word. This Word document format does not support XML.
PDF (.pdf)	Use this format for files you want to share, but do not want to be changed. (Requires Word Add-in).
Web page (.htm, .html)	This format is used to create pages to be viewed on the Web.
Rich Text Format (.rtf)	Many of a document's formatting properties remain, but this file type can be read by more programs.
Plain Text (.txt)	Only text is saved in this file type. Any document formatting is removed.
Word XML Document (.xml)	This file type is used exclusively for XML-enabled documents.

Try saving a document using the instructions below.

We've placed instructions in the appendix of this book on page 171.

I. **MATCHING.**
   Match the correct Word file format to the definition.

1. _G_ a file format that supports macros in Word 2010

2. _H_ format used to create pages viewed on the Web

3. _B_ file type used for XML-enabled documents

4. _E_ default format for Word 2010 documents

5. _F_ formatting is removed—only text is saved in this file type

6. _H_ format for sharing files that will not be changed

7. _D_ format where documents can be read in all versions of Word

8. _C_ file type that can be read by more programs than just Word

A. PDF
B. Word XML Document
C. rich text format
D. Word 97-2003 Document
E. Word Document
F. plain text
G. Word Macro-Enabled Document
H. Web page

Closing a Document

When you're finished using Word 2010, you should exit it. Exiting a program closes it until you need to use it again. Remember that if you click the Close button on the title bar when you have only one Word document open, the document will close and you will exit the Word program.

- Click the File tab and select Close. The document closes, and you can access the file again by opening it later.

Other (and faster) ways to close a document are to press CTRL + W, or to click the X in the top right-hand corner of the document.

Highlights

If you have not saved the document since making changes, a dialog box will appear asking if you want to save changes to the document. Click Save if you wish to save your changes; click Don't Save if you do not want to save your changes; click Cancel if you do not want to close the document.

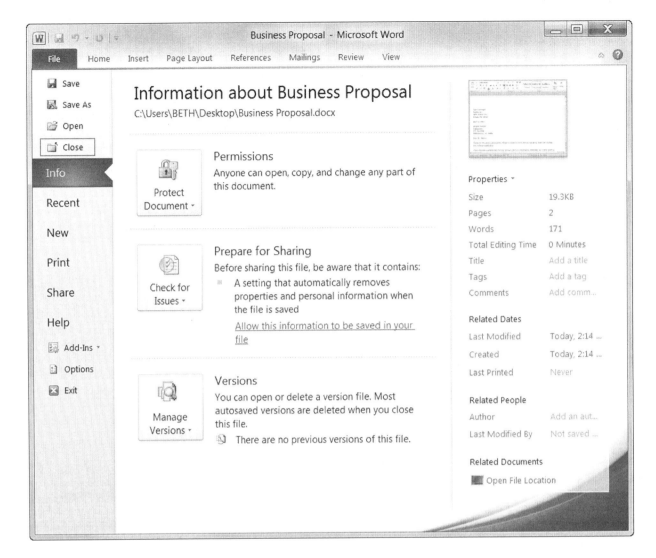

Using Help

When you don't know how to do something in Word 2010, look up your question in the Word Help files. The Word Help files can answer your questions, offer tips, and provide help for all of Word's features.

When a standard search returns too many results, try searching individual sources to narrow things down a bit. Help files have changed in Office 2010. They are still very useful, but the help topics are not as extensive as in previous versions. If you cannot find the help you need you can go to Microsoft Office Discussion Groups which is an online forum where anyone can submit a question and Word experts will answer the question at no cost.

Highlights

Office 2010 offers enhanced ScreenTips for many buttons on the Ribbon. You can use these ScreenTips to learn more about what a button does and, where available, view a keystroke shortcut for the command. If you see the message "Press F1 for more help," press F1 to get more information relative to that command. When you are working in a dialog box, click the Help button to open the Word Help Home page

Help Buttons		
⬅	Back	Click here to move back to the previous help topic.
➡	Forward	Click here to move forward to the next help topic.
✕	Stop	Stop the transfer of information from the online Help database.
↻	Refresh	Refresh the page to correct page layout or get the latest data.
🏠	Home	Click here to return to the Help home page.
🖨	Print	Click here to print the current help topic.
Aᴬ	Change Font Size	Click here to change the size of the text in the Help window.
📖	Show Table of Contents	Click here to browse for help using the Table of Contents.
📌	Keep on Top	Click here to keep the help window on top.

Search for Help

1. Click the Microsoft Word Help button on the Ribbon. The Word Help window will appear. Another way to open the Help window is to press F1.

2. Type what you want to search for in the "Type words to search for" box and press ENTER. A list of help topics will appear.

3. Click the topic that best matches what you're looking for. Word displays information regarding the selected topic.

Enter Search   Browse help topic categories

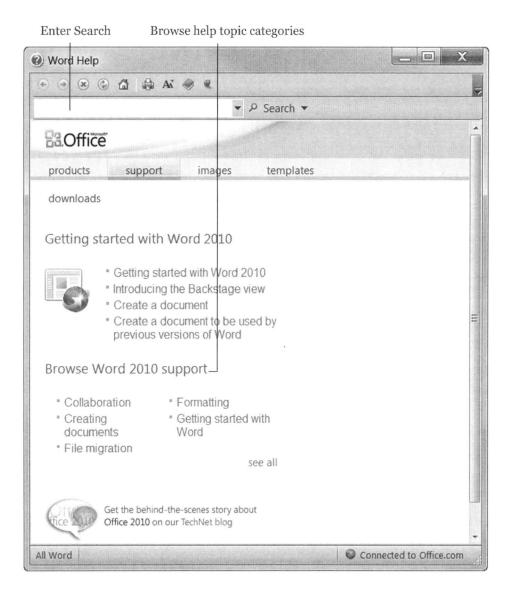

Browse for Help

1. Click the Microsoft Word Help button on the Ribbon. Or, press F1. The Word Help window will appear.

2. Click the category that you want to browse. The topics within the selected category appear. You can click "see all" for a list of all help categories.

3. Click the topic that best matches what you're looking for. Word will display information regarding the selected topic.

Choose the Help source

If you are connected to the Internet, Word 2010 retrieves help from the Office Online database by default. You can easily change this to meet your needs.

1. Click the Search button list arrow in the Word Help window. A list of help sources will appear.

2. Select an option from the list. Now you can search from that source.

I. MULTIPLE CHOICE.
Choose the best answer.

1. What key(s) can you press to get help in Word 2010?
   - ○ ESC
   - ○ CTRL + H
   - ● F1
   - ○ F11

2. If you are connected to the Internet, Word 2010 can retrieve help from the _____.
   - ● Office Online database
   - ○ Online Help database
   - ○ Office Help database
   - ○ none of the above

3. When you search a topic, which help categories are searched?
   - ○ templates and training
   - ○ only templates
   - ○ only training
   - ● all help categories

Exiting Word 2010

When you're finished using Word 2010, you should exit it. Exiting a program closes it until you need to use it again. Exiting or closing a program removes it from the computer's RAM. This frees up RAM for other tasks, such as working with other programs, burning a CD, or anything else that uses your computer's short-term memory.

1. Click the File tab Button.

2. Click the Exit button. The Word program will close.

Click Exit on the File tab to exit document...   ...or click the Close button if there is only one Word document open.

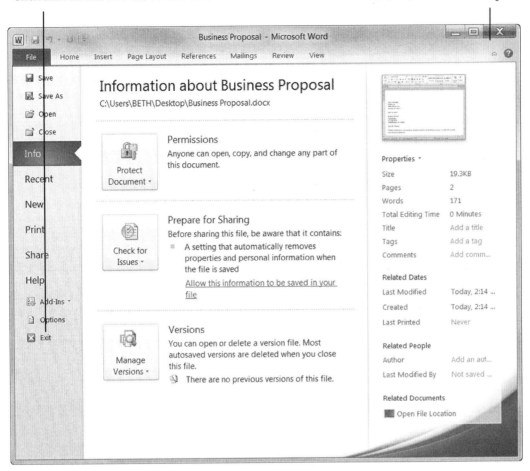

If there is only one Word document open, you can also close the program by clicking the Close button on the title bar. Otherwise, the Close button only closes the document in the window. Having too many programs open at a time could slow down your computer, so it's a good idea to exit all programs that aren't being used.

Highlights

If you have not saved the document since making changes, a dialog box will appear asking if you want to save changes to the document. Click Save if you wish to save your changes; click Don't Save if you do not want to save your changes; click Cancel if you do not want to close the document.

Unit 3
Document Basics

Document Basics – Introduction

When you work with Word, you are working with documents, whether they are letters, memos, or envelopes; any file that is created in Word is called a document. You can do many great things with a document, but before you get into some of the more fun tasks like formatting, you need to learn more basic tasks, like how to create a document and insert text.

This unit will teach you the most basic commands and functions you can perform in Word, such as how to create, open, save, and close a document. It will also go through the most basic commands for working with text, such as inserting and deleting, selecting, and replacing text.

Inserting and Deleting Text

Inserting and deleting text is one of the most important tasks you need to learn how to do in Word. Use the Click and Type feature to enter text in a blank area of the document. Double-click a blank area of the document where you want to position your text and start typing.

Press the ENTER key to start a new paragraph or insert an empty line.

Insert text

Click the insertion point where you want to enter the text and then type the text you want to enter.

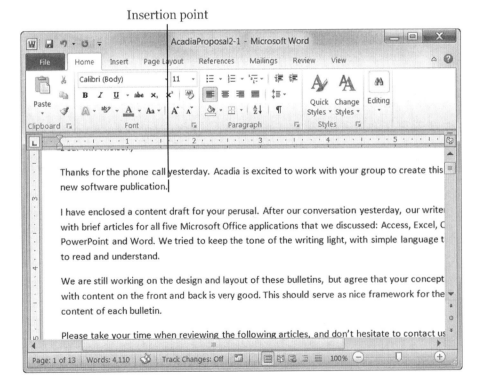

Insertion point

I☰   Double-click near the left side of the page to align text to the left of the page.

I   Double-click near the center of the page to center text over the page.
☰

☰I   Double-click near the right side of the page to align text to the right of the page.

Delete text

To delete a single character: Place the insertion point next to the text that you want to delete. Press the DELETE key to delete text after, or to the right of, the insertion point. Press the Backspace key to delete text before, or to the left of, the insertion point.

To delete a block of text: Select the text you want to delete and press DELETE or Backspace.

Try inserting and deleting some text!

You will need to access practice files in your course online for this lesson. We've placed instructions in the appendix of this book on page 172.

Selecting and Replacing Text

The greatest advantage to using a word-processor is how easy it is to edit text throughout the document. A quick and easy way to edit text is by selecting text and replacing text.

Select text

Selecting text is a very important skill in Word. Whenever you want to work with text to edit or format it, you first need to select it.

1. Click the insertion point at the beginning or end of the text you want to select. Selecting text is a useful skill because once text is selected, you can work with it by replacing, deleting, or formatting it.

2. Click and hold the left mouse button and drag the insertion point across the text. Release the mouse button once the text is selected.

Other ways to select text include the following:

Keystrokes: Press and hold the SHIFT key while using the arrow keys to select characters (Right and Left arrow keys) or lines (Up and Down arrow keys). Add the CTRL key to select by words (Right and Left arrow keys) and paragraphs (Up and Down arrow keys).

Multiple blocks: Select the first block of text and hold down the CTRL key as you select the remaining block(s) of text.

June Cartwright
Acadia, Inc.
3079 Indiana Ave.
Omaha, NE 58712

January 17, 2007

Stephen Nielsen
TechLeaders
P.O. Box 8940
Williamsburg, VA 10089

Dear Mr. Nielsen,

Thanks for the phone call yesterday.
new software publication.

Text with similar formatting: This command selects any text that has the same formatting properties as text that is currently selected. Click the Select button in the Editing group of the Home tab in the Ribbon and select Select Text with Similar Formatting. All text that is formatted exactly as the current text is selected.

Text Selection Shortcuts	
A word	Double-click the word.
Several bits of text	Select the first block of text, then press and hold CTRL as you select the remaining blocks of text.
A sentence	Press and hold CTRL and click anywhere in the sentence.
A line of text	Click in the selection bar next to the line.
A paragraph	Triple-click in the paragraph, or double-click in the selection bar next to the paragraph.
The entire document	Triple-click in the selection bar, or press and hold CTRL and click anywhere in the selection bar, or press CTRL + A, or click the Select button in the Editing group of the Home tab in the Ribbon and select Select All.

Replace text

Replacing text is simple. Do what you learned to select text, then while the text is still highlighted, simply type the new text. The text will be replaced by whatever you choose to type.

Using the instructions below, practice selecting and replacing text.

> You will need to access practice files in your course online for this lesson. We've placed instructions in the appendix of this book on page 173.

   I.   **FILL IN THE BLANK.**
        Review the text selection shortcuts by filling in the blanks below.

   1.   Selecting the first block of text, then pressing and holding CTRL as you select the remaining

        blocks of text will select _Several Bits of text_

   2.   One way to select _Everything_ *(the entire document)* is to press CTRL + A.

   3.   To select a _line of text_ , click in the selection bar next to it.

   4.   A _paragraph_ can be selected by triple-clicking in it or double-clicking in the selection bar next to it.

Navigating through a Document

As a document gets longer, it gets harder and harder to navigate through it. For example, if you were working on a 200-page novel, how would you get to the very end of the document or to page 54? This lesson shows you several ways to navigate through your documents.

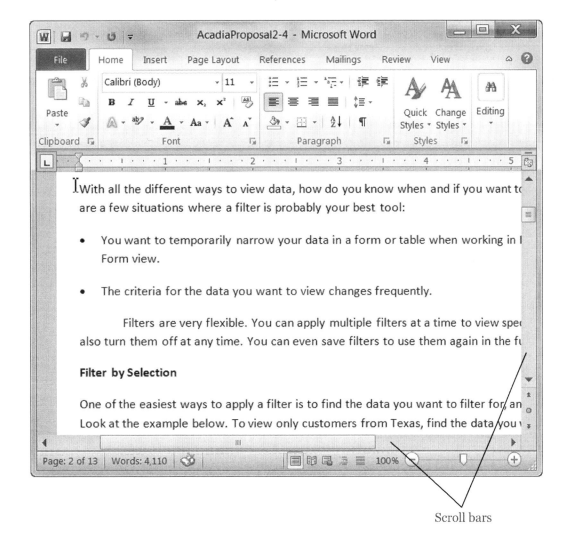

Scroll bars

Scroll bars

The scroll bars are the most basic way to move between pages in a document. The vertical scroll bar is located along the right side of the window and is used to move up and down in a document. The horizontal scroll bar is located along the bottom of the window and is used to move from left to right when a document doesn't fit entirely on the screen.

- When you click the arrow, the screen scrolls down one line at a time. Click and hold to move faster.
- Click and drag the scroll box to move in the document.

Navigation keystrokes

You can use keystrokes to move the insertion point in the document.

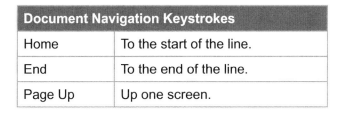

Document Navigation Keystrokes	
Home	To the start of the line.
End	To the end of the line.
Page Up	Up one screen.

Page Down	Down one screen.
CTRL + Home	To the beginning of the document.
CTRL + End	To the end of the document.

Go To

You can move directly to a certain location in the document using the Go To command.

1. Click the Home tab on the Ribbon and click the Find button list arrow in the Editing group. A list of options will appear.

2. Select GO TO from the list. The Find and Replace dialog box will appear.

   Other ways to open the Go To dialog box: press CTRL + G, or press F5.

Highlights

The Go To command can jump to more than just pages. For example, you can jump to a specific heading or footnote in the document. Just select what you want to go to in the "Go to what" list and enter the information in the text box.

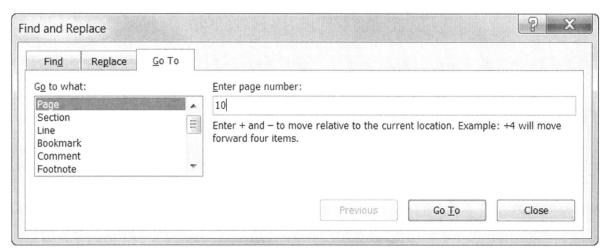

I. **MATCHING.**
   Match the correct term to the definition.

1. _D_ the most basic way to move between pages in a document

2. _C_ moves the insertion point to the beginning of the line

3. _A_ allows you to move directly to a specified page in a document

4. _B_ can be used to move the insertion point in the document

A. Go To command
B. navigation keystrokes
C. Home
D. scroll bars

Browsing a Document

Scrolling through a long document looking for something specific can be both confusing and time-consuming. Word 2010 includes some tools to make browsing longer documents easier.

Browse by object

Browsing by objects allows you to focus on specific aspects of a document as you navigate through it. For example, if you want to focus on how the images look in the document, select Browse by Graphic to quickly jump to each graphic in the document.

1. Click the Select Browse Object button on the vertical scroll bar. When you point to a Browse option, a brief description of that option will appear beneath the options. Another way to open Browse by Object is to press ALT + CTRL + Home.

2. Select the object by which you want to navigate in the document.

3. Click the Previous and Next buttons to navigate through the document. Other ways to Browse Back and Forth Between Objects: Press CTRL + Page Up to go to the previous object, or, press CTRL + Page Down to go to the next object.

Browse by heading

The Navigation Pane makes it easy to get from one place to the next in a document using its headings.

Just remember that headings only appear if you are viewing a document that uses heading styles.

1. Click the View tab on the Ribbon and click the Navigation Pane check box in the Show group. The Navigation Pane will appear, displaying the "Browse the headings in your document" tab. Other ways to open Browse by Object include pressing CTRL + F, or clicking the Home tab and clicking the Find button.

2. Click a heading. The heading is displayed in the main document window.

Browse by page

You can also view thumbnails of all the pages in your document in the Navigation Pane.

3. Click the View tab on the Ribbon and click the Navigation Pane check box in the Editing Show group. The Navigation Pane will appear, displaying the Browse the headings in your document tab. Other ways to open Browse by Object include pressing CTRL + F, or clicking the Home tab and clicking the Find button.

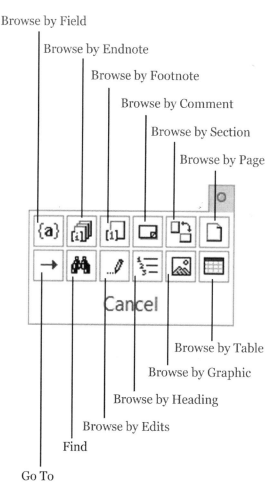

4. Click the Browse the pages in your document tab in the Navigation Pane. Thumbnails of a document's pages appear.

Tip: Use the scroll bar in the Navigation Pane to move through all the pages in a document.

Take a minute to browse around a document!

> You will need to access practice files in your course online for this lesson. We've placed instructions in the appendix of this book on page 174

Viewing a Document

There are several ways to change how a document's contents are displayed on a screen using Document Views. You can also zoom in or out to view more or less of the page at a time, and display hidden document content.

Document Views

Click the View tab on the Ribbon and click the button of the view you want to use in the Document Views group. The document's contents are shown in the selected view. Another Way to Change Document View is to click the button for the view you want to use in the status bar of the document window.

Word offers several different document views:

Print Layout view: This view displays your document as it will appear when printed and is best for working in documents with images. Print Layout view uses more memory and can be slower on older computers.

Full Screen Reading view: This view is optimized for reading. Only necessary toolbars appear, making room for enlarged text and navigational tools.

Web Layout view: Use Web Layout view when you are creating a web page or a document that is viewed on the Web. In Web Layout view, you can see backgrounds, text is wrapped to fit inside the window, and graphics are positioned just as they are in a Web browser.

Outline view: Displays your document in classic outline form. Work in Outline view when you need to organize and develop the content of your document.

Draft view: This view is good for most simple word-processing tasks, such as typing, editing, and formatting. This view does not display advanced formatting, such as page boundaries, headers and footers, or floating pictures.

Zoom

Sometimes it is helpful to make a document appear larger on the computer's screen, especially if you have a small monitor or poor eyesight. It can also be helpful to zoom out so that you can see how the whole document looks.

Click and drag the Zoom slider on the status bar to the percentage zoom setting you want. You could also click the View tab on the Ribbon and click the Zoom button in the Zoom group. Or, click the One Page, Two Pages, and Page Width buttons in the Zoom group.

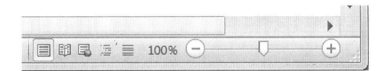

Display and hide hidden characters

Sometimes it is useful to see characters that are normally hidden, such as spaces, tabs, and returns.

Show/Hide Button

1. Click the Home tab on the Ribbon.
2. Click the Show/Hide button in the Paragraph group.

The hidden characters (characters that normally don't print) will appear in the document. Paragraph marks appear as ¶, tabs appear as →, and spaces appear as ·. Notice the Show/Hide button on the Standard toolbar will be highlighted orange, indicating that all the hidden characters in the document are visible.

Displaying hidden characters.

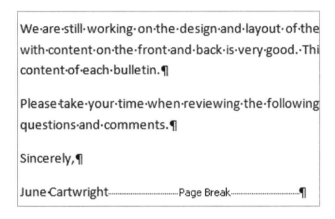

Try out your new viewing techniques.

You will need to access practice files in your course online for this lesson. We've placed instructions in the appendix of this book on page 175.

I. MULTIPLE CHOICE.
Choose the best answer.

1. This view is good for most simple word-processing tasks, such as typing, editing, and formatting.
    - ○ print layout view
    - ◉ draft view
    - ○ outline view
    - ○ full screen reading view

2. Which of following is NOT a way to zoom?
    - ○ Click the View tab, then click the Zoom button.
    - ○ Click and drag the Zoom slider on the status bar to the percentage zoom setting you want.
    - ◉ Select the whole document, then click CTRL + Z.
    - ○ Click the One Page, Two Page, and Page Width buttons.

3. Hidden characters can include _____.
    - ○ tabs
    - ○ spaces
    - ○ paragraph marks
    - ◉ all the above

4. The full screen reading view _____.
    - ◉ optimizes the screen for reading, making room for enlarged text and naviational tools
    - ○ displays your document in classic outline form good for organizing the content of your document
    - ○ displays your document as it will appear when printed
    - ○ lets you see backgrounds and makes the text wrap to fit inside the window

Working with the Document Window

Each document you open in Word has its own window. This window has its own features you can use to change how you work with the document on your Windows desktop.

Change window size

You can change the size of the windows to better organize the space on your screen.

Maximize/Restore Down: When the document window is at its full size, this button will appear as the Restore Down button. When the window will appear in a smaller size, the button will appear as the Maximize button.

Minimize a Window: Click the Minimize button on the title bar. Or, click the document's button on the Windows taskbar.

Resize a Window: Click and drag the resize control in the lower-right corner of the window.

Split the Document Window

Splitting the document window is a great way to view two parts of one document at the same time. When the window is split, you can make changes to the document as you would normally.

1. Click the View tab on the Ribbon and click the Split button in the Window group. A gray shaded line will appear in the document window with a cursor.

2. Click where you want to split the document window. The document window is split into two panes. Now you can scroll up and down in each pane to view different parts of the document at the same time.

   Another way to do this is to place your cursor on the line above the View Ruler button on the vertical scroll bar. When the cursor changes to $\frac{\div}{\div}$, click and drag down to split the window in two. When you no longer want the window to be split, remove the split.

3. Click the View tab on the Ribbon and click the Remove Split button in the Window group. The window is no longer split. Another way to remove a document split is to click and drag the split line to the top or bottom of the document area.

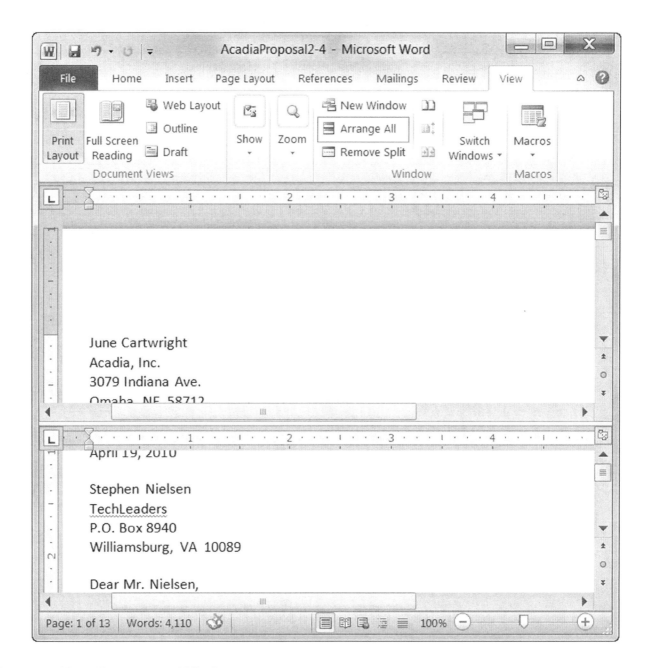

Create a New Document Window

You can view the same document in more than one window at a time. Click the View tab on the Ribbon and click the New Window button in the Window group. Another window opens with the document's contents.

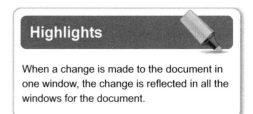

Highlights

When a change is made to the document in one window, the change is reflected in all the windows for the document.

It is important to understand that viewing a document in multiple windows does not create a new file. Any changes made in one of the document windows are applied to the same file. When a change is made to the document in one window, the change is reflected in all the windows for the document. Each instance of a document window is marked in the title bar. For example, if a new window was opened for Document 1, the two document windows would be named Document 1:1 and Document 1:2.

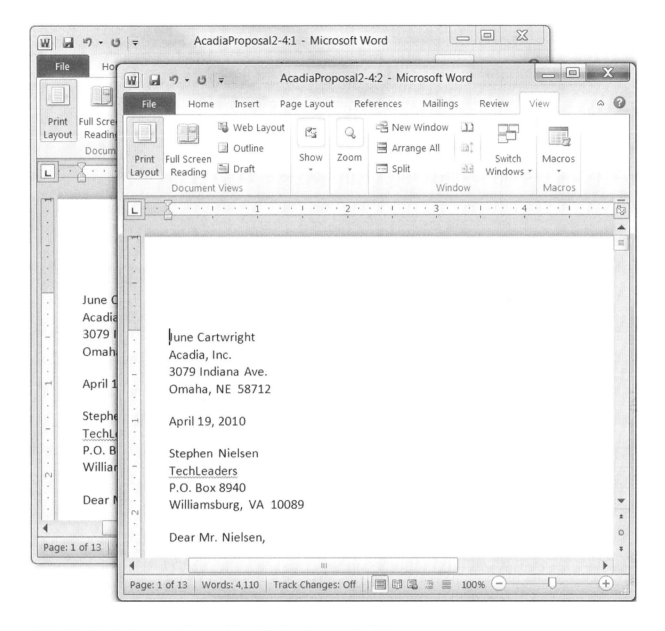

Using the files below, practice working with the document window.

You will need to access practice files in your course online for this lesson. We've placed instructions in the appendix of this book on page 176.

Viewing Multiple Document Windows

Since each document has its own window, you can work with the windows and view several document windows at the same time. Of course the higher your screen resolution, the more windows that can be accommodated.

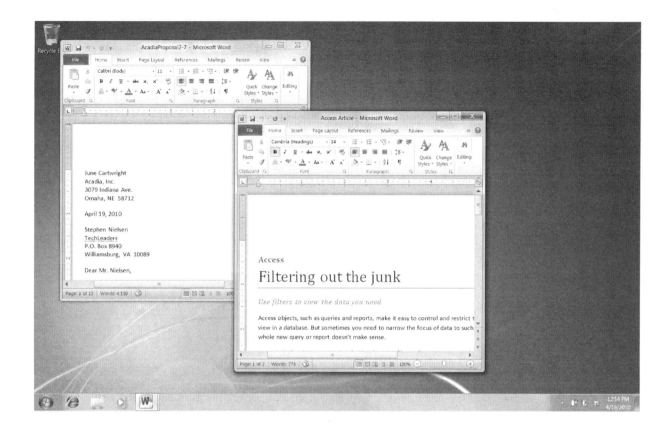

Switch Between Document Windows

If you have several documents open in Word, you can switch between them while still having them open.

1. Point to the Word program button on the Windows taskbar. A preview of all open document windows appear.
2. Click the preview for the document window you wish to open. The selected document window becomes the active document.

Tip: Other ways to switch to another document window include clicking the View tab on the Ribbon and then clicking the Switch Windows button in the Window group. Select the document you want to view.

Arrange Document Windows

Click the View tab on the Ribbon and click the Arrange All button in the Window group. The document windows are tiled on top of each other, stacked horizontally, so that they can be viewed at the same time, but as separate windows.

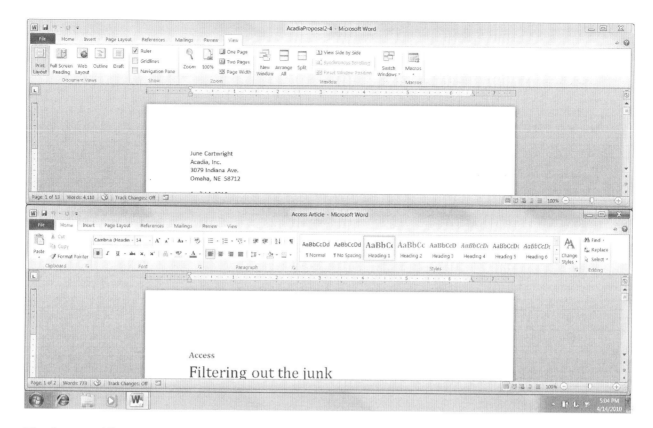

The Arrange All command arranges all document windows that are currently open. The number of document windows that can be arranged on the screen at one time depends on your screen resolution. A higher screen resolution can accommodate more windows.

To view more of a document window's contents at a time, have as few documents open at a time as possible. Only open the documents that you need so you can view more of their contents at a time.

Compare Documents Side By Side

If you need to compare the contents of documents to each other, one of the best ways to do this is to view them side by side.

1. Open the two documents you want to view side by side. The active document will be compared with another open document of your choice.

2. Click the View tab and click the View Side by Side button in the Window group.
   If only two documents are open, the documents are shown side by side.

Highlights

The View Side by Side feature only works with two document windows. If more than two documents are open, the Compare Side by Side dialog box will appear. Click the document you want to view alongside the active document and click OK.

   Synchronous Scrolling is activated by default. This allows you to scroll down both windows at the same time.

   Reset Window Position adjusts the size of the windows so that they share the screen equally.

3. Click the View Side by Side button to turn off Compare Side by Side. Only the active window is shown, while the other document will remain open.

Take a minute to try viewing multiple document windows.

You will need to access practice files in your course online for this lesson. We've placed instructions in the appendix of this book on page 177

I. FILL IN THE BLANK.
Enter the correct word in the blank provided.

1. The View Side by Side feature does not work with more than ___two___ document windows.

2. The control that allows you to scroll down both windows at the same time is called

   Synchronous. Scrolling

3. The ___higher___ your screen resolution, the more windows that can be accommodated.

4. When a document window is ___active___, it is currently available to be worked on.

Unit 4
Working With and Editing Text

Working With and Editing Text – Introduction

Word can do a lot of things, but its primary function is to be a word processor. It can help you out with anything that has to do with words. It's also the most popular program for creating letters, memos, reports, outlines—any document that is primarily focused on producing text.

Since text is the primary function and purpose of Word, this unit deals with how to work with text when you insert and edit it in the document.

Checking Spelling and Grammar

Part of editing your documents is making sure that everything is spelled and put together correctly. Word is a great help in this regard, because it can identify spelling and grammar errors in your documents.

The spell checker is a great feature for catching words that are *spelled* incorrectly, but it will not catch words that are *used* incorrectly. For example, if you typed the word "hat" when you meant to type "had," Word wouldn't catch it because "hat" is a correctly spelled word.

Check spelling and grammar in the document

To check the spelling and grammar of a document all at once, use the Spelling and Grammar dialog box.

1. Click the Review tab on the Ribbon and click the Spelling and Grammar button in the Proofing group. Word will begin checking spelling and grammar from the location of the insertion point. Another way to Check Spelling and Grammar is to press F7.

   If Word finds an error, the Spelling and Grammar dialog box will appear with the error in the text box at the top of the dialog box. See the table below for more information about the different options in the dialog box.

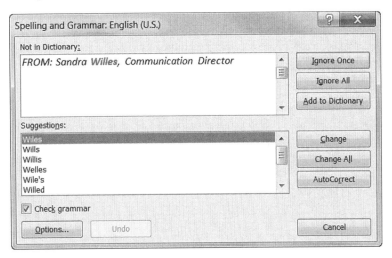

Spelling and Grammar Options	
Ignore Once	Accepts the spelling or grammar you used.
Ignore All or Ignore Rule	Accepts the spelling or grammar you used and ignores all future occurrences in the document.
Next Sentence	Skips the grammar error and goes on to the next one
Add to the Dictionary	If a word is not recognized in the Microsoft Office Dictionary, it is marked as misspelled. This command adds the word to the dictionary so it is recognized in the future.
Change	Changes the spelling of the word to the spelling that is selected in the Suggestions list.
Change All	Changes all occurrences of the word in the document to the selected spelling. Exercise caution when using this command: you might end up changing something you didn't want to change.

2. If the word or grammar is incorrect, select the correction from the Suggestions list, or type your own correction in the top text box. Then click Change or Change All. If the word or grammar is correct, click Ignore Once, Ignore All, Next Sentence, or Add to Dictionary. Word applies the command and continues to the next error. Once Word has finished checking your document for spelling and grammar errors, a dialog box will appear.

3. Click OK to complete the check. You can turn off spell and grammar checker. Click the File tab and click the Options button. Click the Proofing tab. Click the Check spelling as you type check box and/or the Mark grammar errors as you type check box. Click OK.

Correct a single error

By default, Word checks for spelling and grammar errors as you type, underlining misspelled words in red and grammar errors in green. This makes it easy to find and correct errors individually.

1. Right-click the error. A contextual menu will appear, suggesting possible corrections.

2. Select a correction from the contextual menu. Word corrects the error, and the red or green underline will disappear. On the other hand, if something is underlined in red or green but you know it is correct, you can get rid of the underline by selecting Ignore, Ignore All, or Add to Dictionary from the contextual menu.

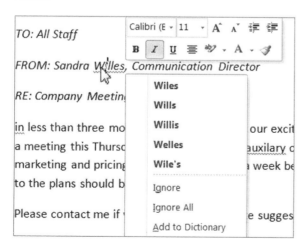

Use contextual spell check

Is it "there," "their," or "they're"? "It's" or "its"? Sometimes a word's spelling depends on its meaning: this is called contextual spelling. You can enable contextual spell check so that Word takes meaning into account when checking your work.

1. Click the File tab and click the Options button. The Word Options dialog box will appear.

2. Click the Proofing tab. The Proofing tab lists options related to editing and proofreading your document.

3. Click the Use contextual spelling check box. This option is listed under the "When correcting spelling and grammar in Word" heading.

4. Click OK. Word will check a word's context during spell check. Contextual spelling errors will be underlined in blue.

Check a little spelling using the files below.

Grammar error   Spelling error

in less than three months, we will introduce our
a meeting this Thursday at 9:30 A.M. in the auxilary
marketing and pricing plans. We are nearly a week
to the plans should be submitted by Friday.

Please contact me if their are any last minute

Contextual spelling error

There are many possible contextual spelling errors, and Word cannot catch all of them. You should always proofread a document to make sure your work is accurate.

You will need to access practice files in your course online for this lesson. We've placed instructions in the appendix of this book on page 178.

I. **MULTIPLE CHOICE.**
    Choose the best answer.

1. The Ignore All or Ignore Rule option _____.
    - ● skips the grammar error and goes to the next one
    - ○ changes all occurrences of the word to the selected spelling
    - ○ changes the spelling of the word to the spelling that is selected in the Suggestions list
    - ○ accepts the spelling or grammar you used and ignores all future occurrences in the document

2. Word begins checking spelling and grammar _____.
    - ○ at the beginning of the document
    - ● from the location of the insertion point
    - ○ at the end of the document
    - ○ none of the above

3. Which errors will Word catch?
   - ⊙ misspellings and grammatical errors
   - ○ misuses of words
   - ○ only grammatical errors
   - ○ only misspellings

4. Grammar errors are underlined in _____.
   - ○ red
   - ○ yellow
   - ⊙ green
   - ○ blue

5. Which option in the Spelling and Grammar dialog box changes the spelling of the word to the spelling that is selected in the Suggestions list?
   - ○ Ignore Once
   - ○ Ignore All/Ignore Rule
   - ⊙ Change
   - ○ Change All

Finding Text

The Navigation Pane is a new feature in Word 2010 that can help you quickly find specific text in a document. You can also access the Find and Replace dialog box from the Navigation Pane if you prefer to use that.

Find text

Use the Navigation Pane to browse, view, and search a document.

1. Click the Home tab on the Ribbon and click the Find button in the Editing group. The Navigation Pane will appear. Other ways to find text include pressing CTRL + F or clicking the View tab and click the Navigation Pane check box in the Show group.

2. Click the Search document text box and enter the text you want to find. The "Browse the results of your current search" tab will appear, displaying your search results. The table to the right, Navigation Pane Tabs, explains each tab of the Navigation Pane.

Find options and additional search

Click a tab to browse a document, view its layout, or view search results

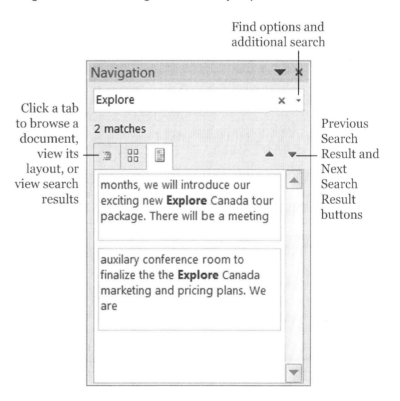

Previous Search Result and Next Search Result buttons

3. Click a result to navigate to it. The result will appear in the main document window. You can also click the Previous Search Result or Next Search Result button to navigate through the document.

4. When you're done, click the Close button. The Navigation Pane closes.

Open the Find and Replace dialog box

Prior to Word 2010, you would have used the Find and Replace dialog box to search the text of a document. You can still access the Find and Replace dialog box from the Navigation Pane.

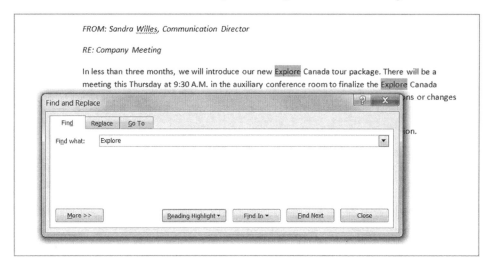

1. Click the Home tab on the Ribbon and click the Find button in the Editing group. The Navigation Pane will appear. Another way to find text it to either press CTRL + F, or, click the View tab and click the Navigation Pane check box in the Show group.

2. Click the Search document text box and enter the text you want to find. The Browse the results of your current search tab will appear, displaying your search results.

3. Click the Find options and additional search commands button and select Replace from the list. The Find and Replace dialog box opens. Click the Find tab.

4. (Optional) Choose what you want to do with text that matches your find request:

   Reading Highlight: Click the button to select "Highlight All," which highlights each instance of the word or phrase in the document.

   Find in Options:

   Current Selection: Search for the text within the currently selected text.

   Main Document: Search for the text throughout the main document.

   Comments: Search for the text within comment balloons inserted in the document.

   Find Next: Search throught the document one item at a time.

5. When you're finished, click Close.

Tip: Click the Find options and additional search commands button and select Options from the list to view more search options.

Ready to practice finding some text? Use the files below to give it a try!

You will need to access practice files in your course online for this lesson. We've placed instructions in the appendix of this book on page 179

Replacing Text

Don't waste time scanning through your document to find text and replace it with something new. Word's Replace command can do this for you with just a few clicks of your mouse.

Replace text

Replace finds specific words and phrases, and then replaces them with something else.

1. Click the Home tab on the Ribbon and click the Replace button in the Editing group. The Replace tab of the Find and Replace dialog box will appear. You can also press CTRL + H or type the term you wish to replace in the Search document text box of the Navigation Pane, click the list arrow, and select Replace from the list.

2. Click the Find what text box and enter the text you want to be replaced.

3. Click the Replace with text box and enter the replacement text.

4. Click Find Next. The first occurrence of the "Find what" text is highlighted.

5. Choose how you want to replace the text:

   Replace: Click to replace the current item.

   Replace All: Click to replace each item found in the document. Use this command with caution: you might replace something you didn't want to replace.

Search options

Use Word's search options to change how Word searches in the document. To do this, click the More button in the Find and Replace dialog box to specify how to search for text. The table below describes the Search Options available under the Find and Replace tabs.

Highlights

If you specify Search Options, make sure to turn them off when you are finished. Otherwise, subsequent find or replace commands will use the same search options. The table below describes the Search Options available under the Find and Replace tabs.

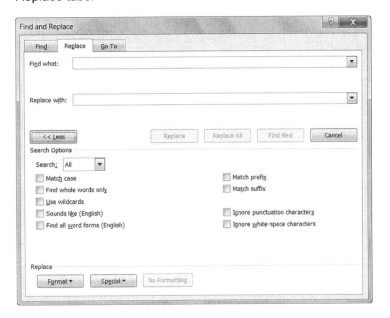

Find and Replace Search Options	
Search	Choose whether to search up, down, or the entire document from the current location.
Match case	Search only for text that matches the capitalization entered.
Find whole words only	For example, if you're looking for "son," selecting this option will skip over words that contain son, such as Hanson, lesson, or sonic.
Use wildcards	Search for wildcards, special characters, or special search operators as added in the "Find what" box. To add wildcards, click Special and select the item, or type the item. If this check box is cleared, Word considers the wildcards and operators to be plain text.
Sounds like (English)	Words that sound the same as the Find what text, but are spelled differently.
Find all word forms (English)	Searches for all forms of the word.
Match prefix	Searches for the text in the Find what box at the beginning of the word.
Match suffix	Searches for the text in the Find what box at the end of the word.
Ignore punctuation	Does not account for punctuation when searching for entered text.
Ignore white-space characters	Does not account for characters that add white space, such as spaces or empty paragraph marks.

Format button	Specify formatting characteristics you want to find attached to the text in the Find what text box.
Special button	Allows you to search by special characters such as Paragraph marks or Em-dashes. Inserts special characters in the "Find what" or "Replace with" boxes.

Give replacing text a try!

You will need to access practice files in your course online for this lesson. We've placed instructions in the appendix of this book on page 180

I. MATCHING.
Match the correct Find and Replace search options to the definition.

1. _G_ Use wildcards
2. _F_ Ignore punctuation
3. _D_ Match prefix
4. _B_ Match case
5. _E_ Special button
6. _H_ Sounds like
7. _A_ Format button
8. _C_ Ignore white-space characters

A. specifies formatting characteristics you want to find attached to the text in the "Find what" text box
B. searches only for the text that matches the capitalization entered
C. does not account for spaces or empty paragraph marks
D. searches for the text in the "Find what" box at the beginning of the word
E. allows you to search by and insert special characters
F. does not account for punctuation when searching for entered text
G. searches for wildcards, special characters, or special search operators as added in the "Find what" box
H. words that sound the same as the "Find what" text, but are spelled differently

Using Word Count and the Thesaurus

Two other tools that are useful in working with text are Word Count and Thesaurus.

Word count

The Word Count feature counts all the words in your document. This is useful if you have a writing assignment that is limited to a number of words, such as a 600-word report.

1. Click the Review tab on the Ribbon and click the Word Count button in the Proofing group. The Word Count dialog box will appear, displaying document information. This includes the number of words, pages, characters, paragraphs and lines.

Highlights

To specify word count to certain areas of the document, select the text you want to include in the count. The number of selected words will appear in the status bar. Use the CTRL key to select non-adjacent text.

A quick and easy way to find out how many words are in a document is via the status bar (left-hand side). The number of words in a document will appear in the status bar by default.

Thesaurus

Use Word's built-in Thesaurus to help you find synonyms for a word. For example, you can use the Thesaurus to replace the ho-hum word "good" with one of its synonyms, such as "commendable," "capital," or "exemplary."

1. Select the word for which you want to find a synonym.

2. Click the Review tab on the Ribbon and click the Thesaurus button in the Proofing group. The Research task pane will appear. You can also right-click a word, point to Synonyms, and select Thesaurus. Or, press SHIFT + F7.

3. Point to the synonym you want to use. Click its list arrow and select Insert. Another way to replace a word with a synonym is to right-click the word for which you want to find a synonym. Point to Synonyms in the contextual menu and select a synonym from the list.

With the help of the files below, try out the word count and thesaurus tools.

You will need to access practice files in your course online for this lesson. We've placed instructions in the appendix of this book on page 181

Inserting Symbols and Special Characters

Your keyboard doesn't contain all the characters you might want to include in your documents. Word lets you insert these special symbols and characters, and even equations, separately.

Insert symbols

You can enter many more characters and symbols in a document than can be found on the keyboard. For example, you can insert the copyright symbol (©), accented and foreign characters (Ç), silly characters (☺), and many more.

1. Place the insertion point where you want to insert the symbol or character.

2. Click the Insert tab on the Ribbon and click the Symbol button in the Symbols group. If you see the symbol you want to use under the Symbol button, select it. Otherwise, open the Symbol dialog box.

3. Select More Symbols. The Symbol dialog box will appear. You can browse the different symbols by changing the Font and Subset of symbols. Special characters such as ellipses are available under the Special Characters tab.

4. Select the symbol you want to use and click Insert. The symbol is inserted into the document.

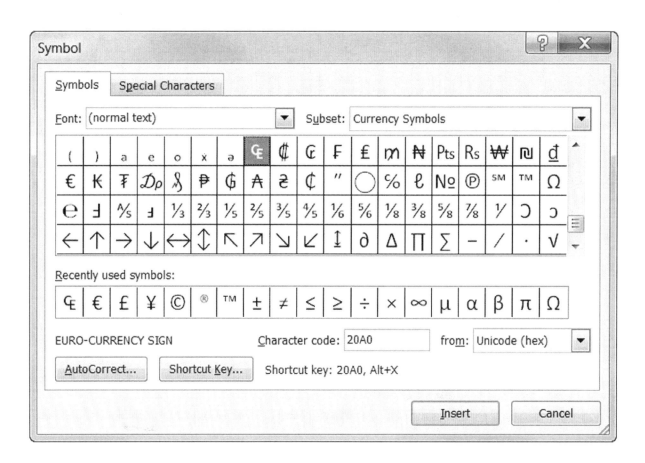

Insert an equation

You may insert a common equation already put together in Word, such as the area of a circle, or $A = \Pi r^2$, or build a new equation using the Equation Design Tools.

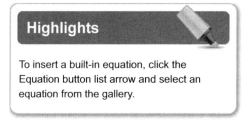

Highlights

To insert a built-in equation, click the Equation button list arrow and select an equation from the gallery.

1. Click the Insert tab on the Ribbon and click the Equation button in the Symbols group. A placeholder for the equation appears in the document, and the Equation Tools appear on the Ribbon. The Design tab is displayed.

   If you want to insert a built-in equation, click the Equation button list arrow and select an equation from the gallery.

2. Type the equation in the placeholder. You may use the keyboard and the Equation Design Tools on the Ribbon to write the equation.

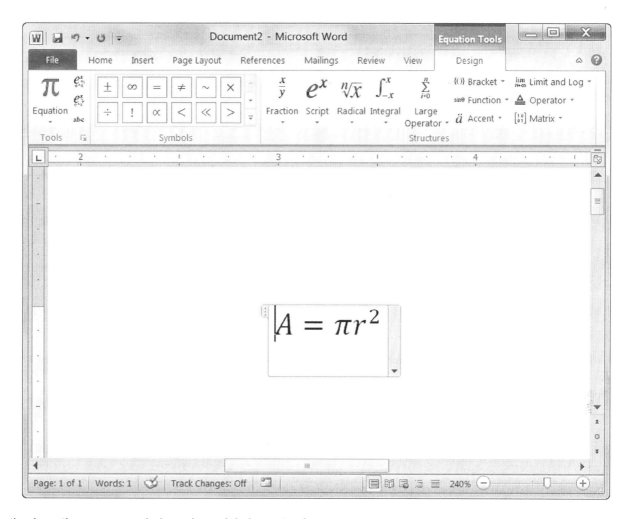

Practice inserting some symbols and special characters!

You will need to access practice files in your course online for this lesson. We've placed instructions in the appendix of this book on page 182.

Copying and Moving Text

You can move or copy text in a Word document by copying or cutting, and then pasting the text in a new place. These commands let you easily work with and rearrange text in the document. The copy and paste commands you will learn on this page will work with all Office programs and most Windows applications. For example, you could copy a name from a Word document and paste it into an Excel worksheet.

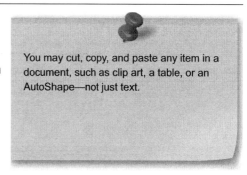

You may cut, copy, and paste any item in a document, such as clip art, a table, or an AutoShape—not just text.

Copy text

When you copy text, the selected text remains in its original location and is added to the Clipboard.

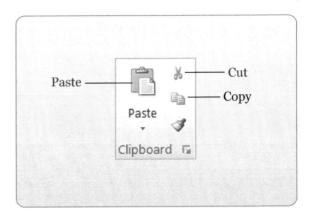

1. Select the text you want to copy.
2. Click the Home tab on the Ribbon and click the Copy button in the Clipboard group. The text is added to the Clipboard, and it remains in the document. Another option is to either press CTRL + C or right-click the selection and select Copy from the contextual menu.
3. Place the insertion point where you want to paste the copied content. The text will be inserted to the right of the insertion point.
4. Click the Home tab on the Ribbon and click the Paste button in the Clipboard group. The copied text is pasted in the new location. You can also simply press CTRL + V or right-click where you want to paste and select Paste from the contextual menu.

Move text

Moving text typically involves a process of cutting and pasting. When you cut text, it is removed from its original location and placed in a temporary storage area called the Clipboard.

1. Select the text you want to move.
2. Click the Home tab on the Ribbon and click the Cut button in the Clipboard group. The text is removed from the document and added to the Clipboard. Another way to move text is to press CTRL + X or right-click the selection and select Cut from the contextual menu.
3. Place the insertion point where you want to paste the content. The text will be inserted to the right of the insertion point.
4. Click the Home tab on the Ribbon and click the Paste button in the Clipboard group. The text is pasted in the new location.

Copy and move text using the mouse

Using the mouse to move and copy cells is even faster and more convenient than using the cut, copy, and paste commands.

1. Select the text you want to move.
2. Point to the selected text.
3. Click and hold the mouse button.
4. Drag the pointer to where you want to move the selected text and then release the mouse button. Pressing and holding the CTRL key while clicking and dragging will allow you to copy the selection.

	Pricing plan final review, 10:45
-	Guest speaker, James McKinsey of Canadian Airways, 11:45
-	Luncheon, 12:00

An overhead display will be available if anyone would like to bring tra
presentations.

Sincerely,

Copying and moving text is easy! Give it a try using the files below.

You will need to access practice files in your course online for this lesson. We've placed instructions in the appendix of this book on page 183.

I. MULTIPLE CHOICE.
Choose the best answer.

1. What is a shortcut for pasting text?
   - ◯ CTRL + X
   - ◯ CTRL + C
   - ◉ CTRL + V
   - ◯ CTRL + P

2. Copying text _____.
   - ◯ removes text from its original location and places it in the Clipboard
   - ◯ removes text from the document and automatically pastes it to the place of your insertion point
   - ◉ selects text that will remain in its original location and adds it to the Clipboard
   - ◯ selects text in the document and moves it to the place of your insertion point

3. You can cut, copy, and paste _____.
   - ◯ text
   - ◯ clip art
   - ◯ tables
   - ◉ all of the above

Controlling How Text is Copied or Moved

You can control how text looks or behaves when it is pasted. For example, you can keep the text's formatting, or have it take on the formatting properties of the destination.

Use paste options

You can control how content is pasted in your spreadsheets using the paste options in Word.

1. Copy or cut an item as you normally would.
2. Click where you want to paste the item.
3. Click the Paste button on the Home tab. Click this button to specify how data is pasted into your worksheet. The content is pasted into the document. The Paste Options button appears in the lower-right corner of the pasted content.
4. Click the Paste Options button. A list of different ways you can paste the content will appear. Or, before pasting, click the Paste button list arrow in the Clipboard group on the Home tab and select a paste option from the list. The options available depend on the type of content being pasted.
5. Point to a paste option. A live preview of how the content will look using that paste option appears.
6. Click a paste option. The text is pasted using the selected option.

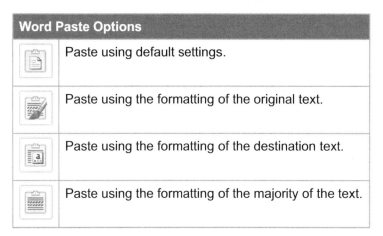

Word Paste Options	
	Paste using default settings.
	Paste using the formatting of the original text.
	Paste using the formatting of the destination text.
	Paste using the formatting of the majority of the text.

Use paste special

You can further control how content is pasted using the Paste Special command.

1. Copy or cut an item as you normally would.
2. Click where you want to paste the item.
3. Click the Home tab and click the Paste button list arrow in the Clipboard group. Now open the Paste Special dialog box.
4. Select Paste Special or press CTRL + ALT + V. The Paste Special dialog box will appear. The options in the Paste Special dialog box depends on the type of content being pasted.
5. Select a paste option and click OK. The content is pasted into the document using the selected option.

The schedule for the meeting is as follows:

- President's introduction, 9:30

- Marketing plan final review, 9:45

- Pricing plan final review, 10:45

- Guest speaker, James McKinsey of Canadian Airways, 11:45

Practice controlling how text is copied and moved.

You will need to access practice files in your course online for this lesson. We've placed instructions in the appendix of this book on page 184

Using the Office Clipboard

If you do a lot of cutting, copying, and pasting you will appreciate the Office Clipboard. The Clipboard lets you collect multiple cut or copied items at a time, which you can then paste as needed. You can even use it to collect and paste items from other Office programs. It should be noted that while the Clipboard is displayed, each cut or copied item is saved to the Clipboard. If the Clipboard is not displayed, the last cut or copied item is replaced by the next one.

Highlights

To remove an item from the Clipboard, click the item's list arrow and select Delete. Click the Clear All button in the task pane to remove all items from the Clipboard.

1. Click the Home tab on the Ribbon and click the Dialog Box Launcher in the Clipboard group. The Clipboard task pane appears along the left side of the window.

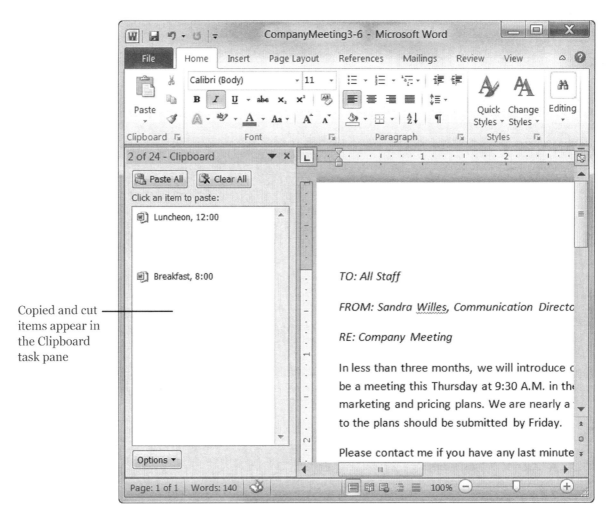

Copied and cut items appear in the Clipboard task pane

2. Cut and copy items as you normally would. The Clipboard can hold 24 items at a time. The icon next to each item indicates the program the item is from. The table below has examples of some common icons.

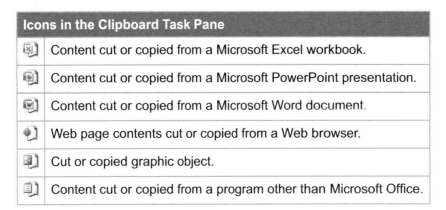

Icons in the Clipboard Task Pane	
	Content cut or copied from a Microsoft Excel workbook.
	Content cut or copied from a Microsoft PowerPoint presentation.
	Content cut or copied from a Microsoft Word document.
	Web page contents cut or copied from a Web browser.
	Cut or copied graphic object.
	Content cut or copied from a program other than Microsoft Office.

3. Click where you want to paste an item from the Clipboard.
4. Click the item in the Clipboard.

The Office Clipboard is quick and easy to use! Practice using it with the files below.

You will need to access practice files in your course online for this lesson. We've placed instructions in the appendix of this book on page 185

Using Undo, Redo, and Repeat

You don't need to be afraid of making a mistake in Word because you can use the Undo feature to erase your actions. The undo, redo, and repeat commands are very useful for working with text in a document.

Undo a single action

Undo does just that—it undoes any actions as though they never happened.

1. Click the Undo button on the Quick Access Toolbar. Your last action is undone. For example, if you had deleted an item and then decided you wanted to keep it after all, undo would make it reappear. The quickest way to undo an action is to press CTRL + Z.

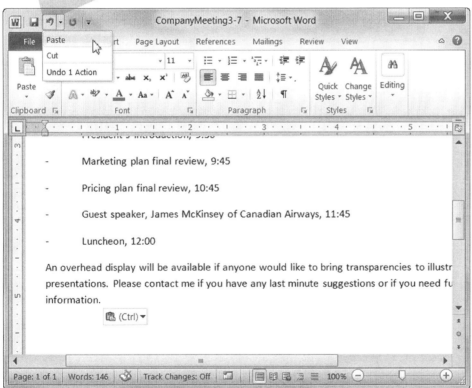

Undo multiple actions

1. Click the Undo button list arrow on the Quick Access Toolbar. A list of the last actions performed in Word will appear. To undo multiple actions, point to the command you want to undo. For example, to undo the last three actions, point at the third action in the list. Each action done before the one you select is also undone. You can undo up to 100 actions in Word, even after saving the document. If you accidentally close the document however, you're out of luck.

2. Click the last action you want to undo in the list. The command you select and all subsequent actions are undone.

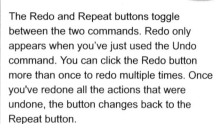

Highlights

The Redo and Repeat buttons toggle between the two commands. Redo only appears when you've just used the Undo command. You can click the Redo button more than once to redo multiple times. Once you've redone all the actions that were undone, the button changes back to the Repeat button.

Redo an action

Redo is the opposite of undo; it redoes an action you have undone. For example, if you decide that you do, after all, want to delete an item that you have just brought back with undo, you can redo the action. This command only appears after you have used the Undo command.

The fastest way to redo an action is to press CTRL + Y.

Repeat an action

Repeat is different from redo because repeat applies the last command to any selected text. For example, rather than applying bold formatting by clicking the Bold button repeatedly, you can repeat the bold command with the Repeat button or keystroke. The Repeat command can also be used to insert text multiple times. For example, you could type a phrase, then click another location in the document, and press F4 to insert the phrase or number.

Repeat button

Take a minute to practice using the undo, redo, and repeat actions.

You will need to access practice files in your course online for this lesson. We've placed instructions in the appendix of this book on page 186

Unit 5

Formatting Characters and Paragraphs

Formatting Characters and Paragraphs – Introduction

You've probably seen documents created by several of your friends or work colleagues and envied their different fonts, italicized and boldfaced type, and fancy paragraph formatting. This chapter explains how to format both characters and paragraphs. You will learn how to change the appearance, size, and color of the characters in your documents. You will also learn the ins and outs of formatting paragraphs: aligning text to the left, right, and center of the page; increasing a paragraph's line spacing; and indenting paragraphs. This unit also describes how to add borders to paragraphs and how to create bulleted and number lists.

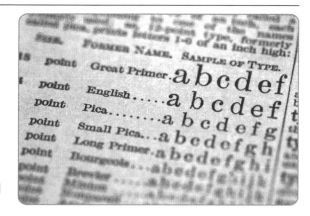

Knowing how to format characters and paragraphs gives your documents more impact and makes them easier to read. Let's get started!

Changing Font Type

One way to emphasize text in a document is by changing its font type. A font type is a set of characters with the same design and shape. As you point to different font types in the Font list, the selected text changes to show you how it will look.

1. Select the text you want to format.
2. Click the Home tab on the Ribbon and click the Font list arrow in the Font group. A list of the fonts that are available on your computer will appear.
3. Select a font from the list. The selected text is changed, and any new text that you enter will appear in the new font type.

Common Font Types	
Calibri	Arial
Times New Roman	Courier
Verdana	Trebuchet MS

Highlights

The font you choose changes the look and feel of a document. For example, a professional document would probably use a more formal font like Times New Roman. On the other hand, a more informal document might use a more friendly font, such as

Andy. Or, if you were writing a report about Egyptian art, you could use the Egyptian-flavored Papyrus font as a heading accent.

Other ways to change font type include the following: When text is selected, click the Font list arrow on the Mini Toolbar. Or, press CTRL + SHIFT + F to open the Font dialog box. Select a font from the Font list and click OK.

It's important to consider the type of document you are creating and the message you are trying to convey when choosing an appropriate font type. For example, Times New Roman might be a better choice than *Curlz* when writing a letter to your boss.

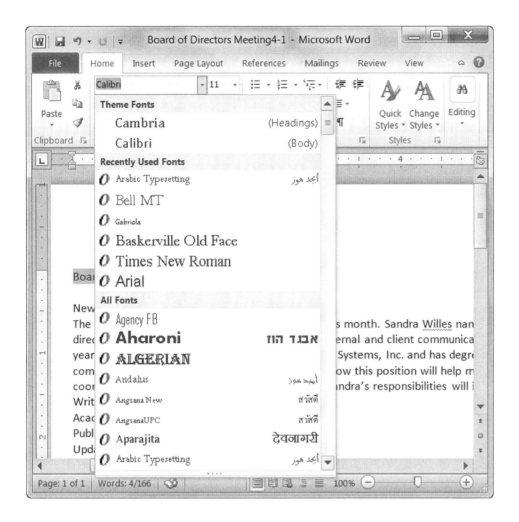

Change a font or two using the instructions below!

You will need to access practice files in your course online for this lesson. We've placed instructions in the appendix of this book on page 187

Changing Font Size

Making text larger is another way to emphasize text.

1. Select the text you wish to format.

2. Click the Home tab on the Ribbon and click the Font Size list arrow in the Font group. A list of font sizes will appear. As you point to different sizes in the Font Size list, the selected text changes to show you how it will look (Live Preview).

3. Select a font size from the list. The selected text will be changed, and any new text that you enter will appear in the new font size.

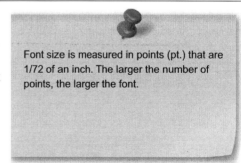

Font size is measured in points (pt.) that are 1/72 of an inch. The larger the number of points, the larger the font.

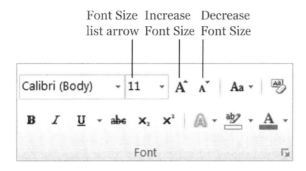

Font Size Increase Decrease
list arrow Font Size Font Size

Other ways to change font size:

- Press CTRL + SHIFT + > to increase font size, and press CTRL + SHIFT + < to decrease font size.
- Click the Font Size list arrow on the Mini Toolbar and select a font size from the list.
- Click the Home tab on the Ribbon and click the Increase or Decrease Font Size button in the Font group.
- Click the Dialog Box Launcher in the Font group, or press CTRL + SHIFT + F to open the Font dialog box. Select a font size from the Font Size list and click OK.

Common Font Sizes	
8 point	Captions, labels
10 point	Large amounts of text
12 point	Large amounts of text
14 point	Subheadings, headings, titles
18 point	Headings, titles

As you point to different sizes in the Font Size list, the selected text changes to show you how it will look.

Ready to change the font size? Use the instructions below to give it a shot.

You will need to access practice files in your course online for this lesson. We've placed instructions in the appendix of this book on page 188.

Changing Font Color and Highlighting Text

Changing font color is yet another way to emphasize text in a document.

Change font color

Unique **font color** makes text stand out against the white background of the document.

The Font Color button always displays the color that was used most recently. To quickly apply this color to other text, simply click the Font Color button—not the list arrow.

1. Select the text you wish to format.

2. Click the Home tab on the Ribbon and click the Font Color button list arrow in the Font group. A list of font colors will appear.

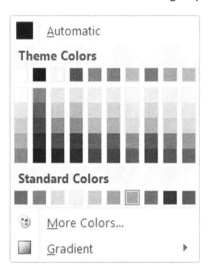

3. Select the color you want to use. The selected text will be changed and any new text that you enter will appear in the new font color. You can also apply a gradient, or gradual color change, to a font. When you select Gradient from the list of font colors, a list of options will appear. Select the gradient you wish to use.

Other ways to change font color are to click the Font Color button list arrow on the Mini Toolbar—this can save a great deal of time. You can also press CTRL + SHIFT + F.

As you point to different colors in the Font Colors list, the selected text changes to show you how it will look. To view more color options, click the Font Color button list arrow and select More Colors.

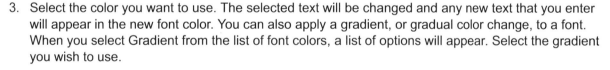

Highlights

If you are using a template or theme, the Font Color list will display only those colors that coordinate with the template or theme. If you don't like any of the available colors, select More Colors from the list to display the Colors dialog box. The Font Color button always displays the color that was used most recently. To quickly apply this color to other text, simply click the Font Color button—not the list arrow. When applying color to text, make sure to keep it subtle. No one wants to stare at neon green text.

Highlight text

Highlighted text changes the background behind text so it looks like a marker was drawn across it.

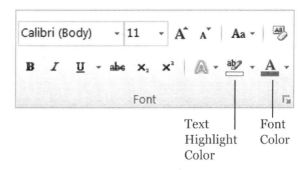

Text Highlight Color

Font Color

1. Click the Home tab on the Ribbon and click the Text Highlight Color button list arrow in the Font group. A list of colors you can use to highlight text will appear.

    Another way to highlight text is to select the text you want to highlight, then click the Text Highlight Color button on the Mini Toolbar.

2. Select the color you want to use. The cursor will change to indicate it is ready for highlighting text.

3. Click and drag the highlight cursor across text you want to highlight. When you no longer want to highlight text, turn off the highlighter.

4. Click the Text Highlight Color button. The highlighter is turned off. Another way to stop highlighting text is to click the Text Highlight Color button list arrow and select Stop Highlighting to remove the highlighting cursor.

To remove text highlighting, click the Text Highlight Color button list arrow and select No Color. Click and drag across highlighted text to remove highlighting.

Try changing font colors and a little highlighting!

You will need to access practice files in your course online for this lesson. We've placed instructions in the appendix of this book on page 189.

Changing Font Styles and Effects

In addition to changing font type, size, and color, you can also emphasize the text in a document by changing the font style and adding font effects. The most common and popular styles are **bold**, *italic*, and underline, but other effects can be applied, such as shadow and ~~strikethrough~~. Text effects are a neat feature, but they may not be suitable for every document. Think about the purpose of the document and the audience that will be reading a document to decide if text effects will enhance your font.

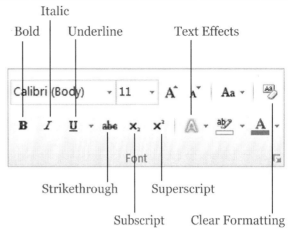

Change font style

1. Select the text you wish to format.

2. Click the Home tab on the Ribbon and click the appropriate button in the Font group. The formatting will apply to the selected text.

3. Another way to change the font style or effect is to select the text you wish to format and click the appropriate button on the Mini Toolbar, or use the keystroke shortcuts listed in the table below. Or, click the Dialog Box Launcher in the Font group, or press CTRL + SHIFT + F to open the Font dialog box and apply formatting.

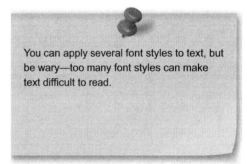

You can apply several font styles to text, but be wary—too many font styles can make text difficult to read.

Add text effects

Using boldface, italics, and underline makes your text stand out but sometimes it's not quite enough. Word 2010 provides even more text effects to add visual impact to your documents.

1. Select the text to you want to format.

2. Click the Home tab on the Ribbon and click the Text Effects button in the Font group. A list of available text effects appears. You can apply one of the available text effects, or you can create your own text effects. You can also click the Home tab on the Ribbon and click the Dialog Box Launcher in the Font group, or press CTRL + SHIFT + F to open the Font dialog box. Click the Text Effects button and select the text effect(s) you wish to use.

3. Select the text effect you wish to use. The text effect is applied.

The table below shows you shortcuts for the most common styles and effects.

Font Styles and Effects Keystroke Shortcuts	
Bold	CTRL + B
Italic	CTRL + I
Underline	CTRL + U
Subscript	CTRL + =
Superscript	CTRL + SHIFT + **+**

Remove font style or effect

To remove a font style or effect, follow the same procedure that you used to apply the style or effect. Or, use the Clear All Formatting button in the Font group.

Ready to switch around some font styles and effects? Use the files below to practice.

> You will need to access practice files in your course online for this lesson. We've placed instructions in the appendix of this book on page 190.

Review: Fonts

I. **MULTIPLE CHOICE.**
   Choose the best answer.

   1. What is NOT the procedure for changing the font type?
      ○ Click the Font list arrow in the Font group of the Home tab.
      ◉ Click the Font list arrow on the Mini Toolbar.
      ◉ Click the Font button on the Formatting tab and select the desired font.
      ○ Open the Font dialog box and select a font from the Font list.

   2. How is font size measured?
      ○ inches or in
      ◉ points or pt
      ○ spikes or sp
      ○ pixels or pi

   3. What is a way to emphasize text?
      ○ change font type
      ○ change font color
      ○ change font size
      ◉ all of the above

   4. What is the shortcut for opening the Font dialog box?
      ○ CTRL + F
      ○ CTRL + B
      ◉ CTRL + SHIFT + F
      ○ CTRL + SHIFT + B

   5. To remove text highlighting, _____.
      ◉ select No Color from the Text Highlight Color button
      ○ press Esc
      ○ click the Home tab on the Ribbon and then the Text Highlight Color button
      ○ click and drag the highlight cursor across text you don't want to highlight and press DELETE

Mark the following true or false.

1. The Font Color button always displays the color that was used most recently.

   ◉ true
   ○ false

2. The Font Color list never displays colors that coordinate with the document theme.

   ○ true
   ◉ false

3. As you point to different colors in the Font Colors list, the selected text changes.

   ◉ true
   ○ false

Applying Spacing and Ligatures

Word allows you to format how individual characters are set in a document. For example, you can adjust spacing between characters or add typographical effects like ligatures to make your document look polished. Word 2010 fonts include a new type of font, OpenType font. Unlike other types of fonts, OpenType fonts support advanced typographical features such as ligatures.

Apply character spacing

You can change the spacing between individual characters.

1. Select the text you wish to format. You can format selected text or a whole document.

2. Click the Home tab and click the Dialog Box Launcher in the Font group. The Font dialog box will appear. You can also right-click the mouse and select Font from the contextual menu. Or, press CTRL + D.

3. Click the Advanced tab. The table below explains the options for character spacing. As you select options, a preview of the formatted text appears at the bottom of the dialog box.

4. Select the option(s) under the Character Spacing heading you want to apply and click OK. The spacing is applied to the text.

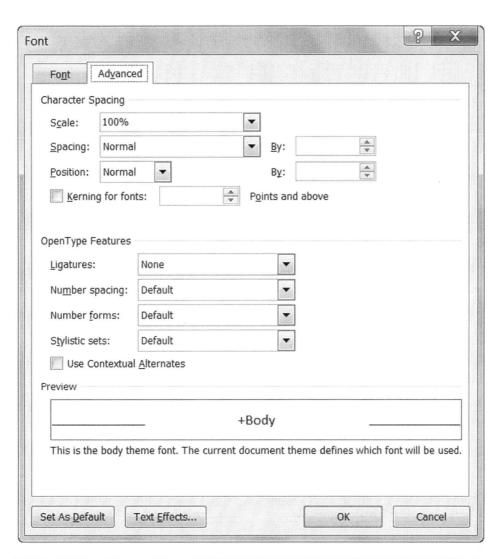

Character Spacing Options		
Scale	Adjusts the width of the characters, but maintains their height.	100%: Office 50%: Office 200%: Office
Spacing	Adjusts the space between characters.	Normal: Office Expanded: O f f i c e Condensed: Office
Position	Adjusts the position of the characters relative to the line.	Normal: Office Raised: Office Lowered: Office
Kerning for fonts	Automatically adjusts the spacing between characters.	Kerning on: **WAR** Kerning off: **WAR**

Apply ligatures

A ligature is a combination of characters written as though they were a single character. Ligatures can add a more professional feel to the document or give it a historical look.

office → office

1. Select the text you wish to format. You can format selected text or a whole document.
2. Click the Home tab and click the Dialog Box Launcher in the Font group. The Font dialog box appears. You may also right-click the mouse and select Font from the contextual menu. Or, press CTRL + D.
3. Click the Advanced tab.
4. Click the Ligatures list arrow. You can select from the following three options:

   Standard only: Uses formally recognized ligatures.

   Standard and Contextual: Uses formally recognized ligatures as well as ligatures that are appropriate for use with the selected font, but that are not standard.

   Historical and Discretionary: Uses historical ligatures that were once standard but are no longer commonly used. Also uses ligatures the font designer included for a specific purpose.

5. Select the ligature option you want to apply and click OK. The ligature is applied to the text.

Open Type Features	
Numbering spacing	**Default:** The default number spacing for the font. **Proportional:** Numbers are spaced with varying widths, much like letters. **Tabular:** Each number has the same width. Select this option when you want numbers to align, such as in a table.
Number forms	**Default:** The default number form for the font. **Lining:** Numbers with the same height that don't extend below the baseline of the text. **Old Style:** The lines of the characters flow above or below the line of the text, making the numbers easier to read.
Stylistic sets	A set of characteristics that changes the look of the text. A font may have up to 20 different style sets.
Use Contextual Alternatives	Select this check box to modify the formatting of letters or combinations of letters based on the surrounding characteristics.

Use the instructions below to try applying ligatures!

You will need to access practice files in your course online for this lesson. We've placed instructions in the appendix of this book on page 191.

Creating Lists

Lists are a great way to present paragraphs of related information. Word will automatically number or continue a list by default. To adjust these options, click the File tab and select Word Options. Click the Proofing tab and click the AutoCorrect Options button. Click the AutoFormat As You Type tab and specify the appropriate options.

Create bulleted and numbered lists

Use bulleted lists when the order of items in a list doesn't matter, such as listing items you need to buy. When the order of items in a list does matter, such as to present step-by-step instructions, try using a numbered list. To choose a different type of bullet or numbering for the list, check the button's list arrow and select a bullet character or numbering scheme from the list.

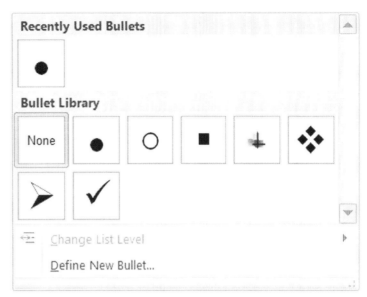

1. Select the lines you want to use for the list. Each line that you want to be bulleted or numbered must appear as its own paragraph.

2. Click the Home tab on the Ribbon and click the Bullets or Numbering button in the Paragraph group. The selected lines are bulleted or numbered. Word includes default bullets and numbering, but you can select another style if you would like.

3. Click the Bullets or Numbering button list arrow and select an option from the library.

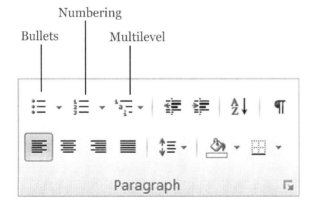

Highlights

To create a new type of bullet or numbering scheme, click the Bullets or Numbering button list arrow and select Define New Bullet or Define New Number Format from the list. Then define the settings in the dialog box.

Create a multilevel list

A multilevel list applies different characters to the levels of text in the document. Outlines and legal documents are examples of multileveled lists.

1. Select the lines you want to include on the list. Each line that you want to be marked must be its own paragraph. Indentations and outline levels will determine the type of character that is applied to a list item.

2. Click the Home tab on the Ribbon and click the Multilevel List button in the Paragraph group. A list of multilevel list types will appear.

3. Select the multilevel list you want to use. The list will be applied to the selected items.

Tip: To create a new type of multilevel list, click the Multilevel List button and select Define New Multilevel List. Then define the settings in the dialog box.

Reset numbering

Numbered lists automatically number each list item in order. However, there are some types of lists where you will need to change a number manually and have Word renumber the items that follow accordingly. You can use this process in a numbered or multilevel list.

1. Right-click the number in the list you want to change. A contextual menu will appear.

2. Select Set Numbering Value from the list. The Set Numbering Value dialog box will appear. There are two options you may use to reset the numbering:

    Start new list: Select this option to start a new list at the number you specify in the "Set value to" box.

    Continue from previous list: Select the "Advance value (skip numbers)" check box and enter the number you wish to begin on in the "Set value to" box.

3. Specify how you want to reset the numbered list and click OK.

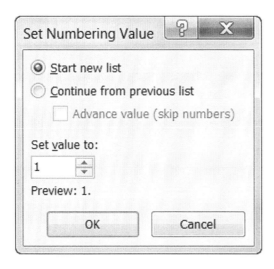

Tip: To remove bullets and numbering from a list select the list and click the Bullets or Numbering button in the Paragraph group on the Ribbon.

Take a minute to try out creating a list.

You will need to access practice files in your course online for this lesson. We've placed instructions in the appendix of this book on page 192.

I. **TRUE/FALSE.**
   Mark the following true or false.

   1. To "Continue from previous list," select the "Advance value" check box and enter the number you wish to begin on in the "Set value to" box.
      - ⦿ true
      - ○ false

   2. A multilevel list does not apply different characters to the levels of text in a document.
      - ○ true
      - ⦿ false

   3. Each line you want to be bulleted or numbered must appear as its own paragraph.
      - ⦿ true
      - ○ false

Changing Paragraph Alignment

While the most common justification is the standard alignment to the left, there are four different alignments in Word: Center, Align Right, Align Left, and Justify. Each alignment can be used to create a different style of text. For example, if you're writing a business letter your text would be aligned to the left. On the other hand, if you are creating a flyer to advertise a yard sale, you might want to use the Center alignment.

Center alignment: Often used in titles, pull quotes, and special layout designs.

Right alignment: Often used when text wraps around objects or for special effects.

Left alignment: Often used in standard paragraphs for ease of reading.

Justified alignment: Often used in presentations and multicolumn pages, such as newsletters.

Complete the following steps to align your text:

1. Place the insertion point in the paragraph you want to change, or (if you want to align more than one) highlight all the paragraphs you want to change.
2. Click the Home tab on the Ribbon and click the Align Left, Center, Align Right, or Justify button in the Paragraph group. The alignment of the paragraph(s) will change.

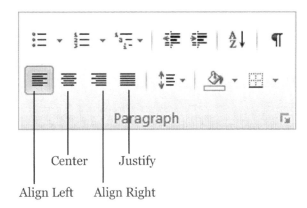

Another way to change paragraph alignment is to click the Dialog Box Launcher in the Paragraph group. On the Indents and Spacing tab in the Paragraph dialog box, click the Alignment list arrow and select and alignment. Click OK.

The table below displays how each alignment might look in a document.

Paragraph Alignments	
Align Left CTRL + L	**New Communications Director** The search for a communications director ended this month. Sandra Willes named communications director and will coordinate and direct all formal internal client communications.
Center CTRL + E	<div align="center">**New Communications Director** The search for a communications director ended this month. Sandra Willes named communications director and will coordinate and direct all formal internal client communications.</div>

Align Right CTRL + R	**New Communications Director** The search for a communications director ended this month. Sandra Willes named communications director and will coordinate and direct all formal internal client communications.
Justify CTRL + J	**New Communications Director** The search for a communications director ended this month. Sandra Willes named communications director and will coordinate and direct all formal internal client communications. Sandra has four years of experience as an office manager at Custom Systems, Inc. and has degree in both marketing and communications.

Using the files below practice changing a paragraph alignment.

You will need to access practice files in your course online for this lesson. We've placed instructions in the appendix of this book on page 193.

Adding Paragraph Borders and Shading

Adding borders and shading to paragraphs can make them more attractive, organized, and easy to read. Borders can be applied in ways that underlining cannot, such as a vertical line or a line above a paragraph.

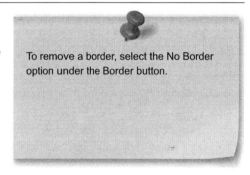

To remove a border, select the No Border option under the Border button.

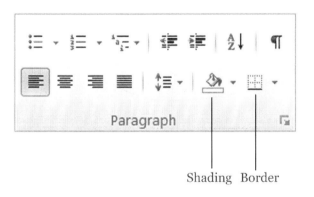

Shading   Border

Add a paragraph border
Borders are lines that you can add to the top, bottom, left, or right of paragraphs. They are especially useful for emphasizing headings.

1. Place the insertion point in the paragraph you want to add the border to. If you want to add the same kind of border to several paragraphs, select them all at once.
2. Click the Home tab on the Ribbon and click the Border button list arrow in the Paragraph group. A list of borders you can add to the selected paragraph(s) appears. Use the examples shown next to each border option to guide your decision. If the border configuration you want doesn't appear in the list, add one border at a time.

3. Select a border type. The border will apply. Notice that the border option you chose will now appear as the selected type on the Border button. If you want to apply the same border to another paragraph, just click the Border button.

⊞	Bottom Border
⊟	Top Border
⊩	Left Border
⊪	Right Border
⊞	No Border
⊞	All Borders
⊡	Outside Borders
⊞	Inside Borders
⊟	Inside Horizontal Border
⊞	Inside Vertical Border
◹	Diagonal Down Border
◸	Diagonal Up Border
⩵	Horizontal Line
📝	Draw Table
▦	View Gridlines
▢	Borders and Shading...

This list of border options appears when you click the Border button list arrow.

Add paragraph shading

Color the background of a paragraph by adding shading. Remember that when you use shading, make sure the shading color complements the font color so the font is readable.

1. Place the insertion point in the paragraph you want to add the shading to. If you want to add the same shading to several paragraphs, select them all at once.
2. Click the Home tab on the Ribbon and click the Shading button list arrow in the Paragraph group. A list of colors that coordinate with the Theme Color that is currently selected will appear.
3. Select the color you want to use. The shading will apply. Notice that the color you chose will appear as the selected color on the Shading button. If the color you want to use does not appear in the list, click More Shading Colors to choose from a larger array of colors. If you want to apply the same shading to another paragraph, just click the Shading button.

Borders and Shading dialog box

The Borders and Shading dialog box is another way to work with borders and shading in paragraphs.

Highlights

If you want to add a pattern to your shading, simply go to the Shading tab of the Borders and Shading dialog box, click the Style list arrow to select a pattern style, and click the Color list arrow to select a pattern color. Easy, right?

1. Select the paragraph(s) to which you want to add borders or shading.
2. Click the Home tab on the Ribbon and click the Border button list arrow in the Paragraph group.
3. Select Borders and Shading from the list. The Borders and Shading dialog box will appear. Here are your options:

    To apply a border: Click the Borders tab and click the side(s) (top, bottom, left, and/or right) of the paragraph in the Preview diagram where you want to apply the borders.

    To apply shading: Click the Shading tab. Click the Fill list arrow and select the color you want to use. When you click the border in the diagram, it will turn the color you selected.

4. Click OK. Word will apply the color to the selected border of the selected paragraph.

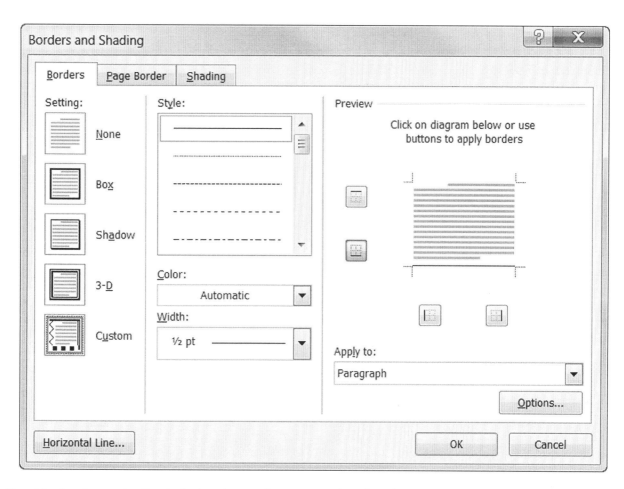

Tip: To add a border or shading to text, not an entire paragraph, select the text and open the Borders and Shading dialog box. Click the Apply to list arrow and select Text. Then specify the border and shading options you want to use.

Using the files below, practice adding paragraph borders and shading!

You will need to access practice files in your course online for this lesson. We've placed instructions in the appendix of this book on page 194.

I. MULTIPLE CHOICE.
Choose the best answer.

1. You can add border lines to the _____ of paragraphs.
   - ◯ top
   - ◯ bottom
   - ◯ right
   - ● all of the above

2. How do you apply shading to a paragraph?
   - ◯ Click the Shading tab, then click the sides of the paragraph in the Preview diagram.
   - ● Click the Shading tab, then click the Fill list arrow and select the color you want to use.
   - ◯ Highlight the paragraph you want to shade, the click on a color directly from the Ribbon tab.
   - ◯ Click in the paragraph you want to shade, then select a border type.

3. To remove a border, you need to _____.
   - ◯ press CTRL + B
   - ◯ delete the whole paragraph
   - ● select the No Border option
   - ◯ click the Undo button

Changing Line Spacing

Adding space between lines makes a document easier to read. Sometimes it will be necessary to create a paper with 1.5 or double spacing so that edits or comments can be made, so it is important to learn how to change line spacing.

Line Spacing

1. Place the insertion point in the paragraph you want to change or select the paragraphs you want to change.

2. Click the Home tab on the Ribbon and click the Line Spacing button in the Paragraph goup. A list of spacing options will appear. Depending on the version of Word, the default line spacing is either 1.0 (Single) or 1.5 (Space-and-a-half).

3. Select the spacing you want to use. The line spacing will apply to the paragraph(s).

Another way to change line spacing is to click Home tab on the Ribbon and click the Dialog Box Launcher in the Paragaph group. On the Indents and Spacing tab, click the Line spacing list arrow and select an option. Click OK.

Line Spacing Options	
Single	Single spacing—line spacing that accommodates the largest font in that line, plus a small amount of extra space. This is the default setting for paragraphs.
1.5 Lines	Space-and-a-half spacing—line spacing for each line that is one-and-one-half times that of single line spacing. For example, if 10-point text is spaced at 1.5 lines, the line spacing is a little over 15 points.
Double	Double-spacing—line spacing for each line that is twice that of single line spacing. For example, in double-spaced lines of 10-point text, the line spacing is a little over 20 points.
At Least	Minimum line spacing that Word can adjust to accommodate larger font sizes that would not otherwise fit within the specified spacing.
Exactly	Fixed line spacing that Word does not adjust. This option makes all lines evenly spaced.
Multiple	Line spacing that is increased or decreased by a percentage that you specify. For example, setting line spacing to a multiple of 1.2 would increase the space by 20 percent, while setting line spacing to a multiple of 0.8 would decrease the space by 20 percent. Setting the line spacing at a multiple of 2 is equivalent to setting the line spacing at Double. In the "At" box, type or select the line spacing you want. The default is three lines.

Practice changing the line spacing of a document using the files below.

You will need to access practice files in your course online for this lesson. We've placed instructions in the appendix of this book on page 195.

Changing Spacing Between Paragraphs

Adding space between the paragraphs in a document gives it structure and makes it easier to read. It is important to understand the difference between line spacing and spacing between paragraphs. They are as they sound—line spacing is how far apart each line is from the other, and spacing between paragraphs is how far apart each paragraph is from the other.

Highlights

To remove paragraph spacing, change the spacing values to 0 pt in the Paragraph dialog box. Or, click the Line Spacing button in the Paragraph group and select Remove Space Before Paragraph or Remove Space After Paragraph. Or, click the Page Layout tab on the Ribbon and adjust the Before and After boxes in the Paragraph group.

1. Place the insertion point in the paragraph you want to change or select the paragraph(s) you want to change.
2. Click the Home tab on the Ribbon and click the Dialog Box Launcher in the Paragraph group. The Paragraph dialog box will appear. You can adjust the space before and after the paragraph:

    Before: Adds space above the paragraph

    After: Adds space below the paragraph

3. Select the spacing you want to use and click OK. The paragraph(s) will change with the paragraph spacing.

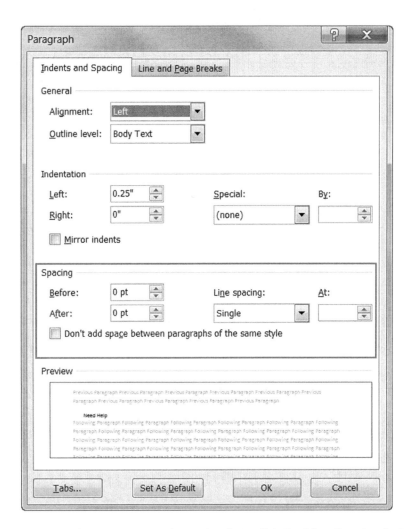

Another way to change paragraph spacing is to click the Line Spacing button in the Paragraph group. Select Add Space Before Paragraph or Add Space After Paragraph. By default, 12 points of space are added in the direction specified.

With paragraph spacing.

Board of Directors Meeting

New Communications Director

The search for a communications director ended this month. Sandra Willes n

director and will coordinate and direct all formal internal and client commun

years of experience as an office manager at Custom Systems, Inc. and has de

Without paragraph spacing.

Sometimes you may want to add a separator between paragraphs. The most common use for this would be to signal to the reader that you are introducing a new idea. To add a horizontal separator, simply hit Enter after the last paragraph you have typed. Type three hyphens in a row, "——", on the new line and hit Enter again. The hyphens will be converted into a solid horizontal line.

Change the spacing between paragraphs using the files below.

> You will need to access practice files in your course online for this lesson. We've placed instructions in the appendix of this book on page 196.

Using the Format Painter

If you find yourself applying the same formatting over and over again, then you should familiarize yourself with the Format Painter tool—it can save you a great deal of time. The Format Painter copics how text is formatted and lets you apply that formatting elsewhere.

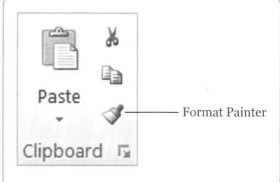

Format Painter

1. Select the text with the formatting you want to copy. The Format Painter will copy character (font color or italics) and paragraph (line spacing, indentation) formatting attributes of the selected text.
2. Click the Home tab on the Ribbon and click the Format Painter button in the Clipboard group. The insertion point changes to a paintbrush. Single-click the Format Painter button to apply copied formatting once. Double-click the Format Painter button to apply copied formatting multiple times.
3. Click and drag the paintbrush across the text to which you want to apply the copied formatting. The copied formatting will apply. Note: To copy paragraph formatting (such as line or paragraph spacing) as well as text formatting, select the entire paragraph you want to copy, then click the Format Painter button.

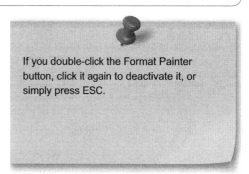

If you double-click the Format Painter button, click it again to deactivate it, or simply press ESC.

Take a minute to practice using the format painter tool.

You will need to access practice files in your course online for this lesson. We've placed instructions in the appendix of this book on page 197.

Setting Tab Stops

Tabs make it easy to align text. Each time you press the TAB key, the insertion point moves to the next tab stop. Word has left tab stops set at every half-inch by default, but you can easily create your own stops to be located in a specific position or using a different alignment.

Tab alignment box

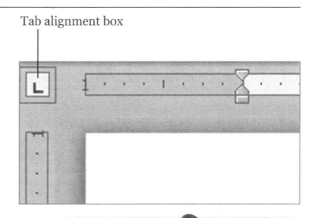

Set tabs with the ruler

The advantage of setting tabs with the ruler is that it is easy to see where the tab is positioned in the document.

1. (If the ruler is not displayed) Click the View tab on the Ribbon and click the Ruler check box in the Show/Hide group. The ruler will appear.
2. Click the Tab alignment box on the ruler until you see the type of tab you want to use (left, center, right, decimal, or bar). The left tab is the default and most common type of tab. However, you can align text differently by using different tabs.
3. Click where you want to add the tab stop on the ruler. A tab of the selected tab alignment type is added to the ruler. Now, when the TAB key is pressed, the cursor will jump to the tab stop where you can now insert text.

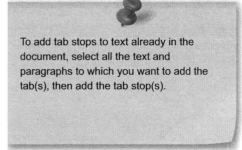

To add tab stops to text already in the document, select all the text and paragraphs to which you want to add the tab(s), then add the tab stop(s).

Set tabs with the Tabs dialog box

The Tabs dialog box is slightly slower to work with than setting tabs with the ruler, but it is more accurate and gives you more options.

1. Click the Home tab on the Ribbon and click the Dialog Box Launcher in the Paragraph group. The Paragraph dialog box will appear.
2. Click the Tabs button near the bottom of the Paragraph dialog box. The Tabs dialog box will appear.
3. Select the alignment, choose the type of leader, and specify the location of the tab stop on the ruler. Once you've selected the tab settings, you're ready to set the tab.
4. Click Set. The tab is created with the specified attributes. Continue adding more tabs here as necessary.
5. Click OK once each tab is set. The tab stops are shown on the Ruler.

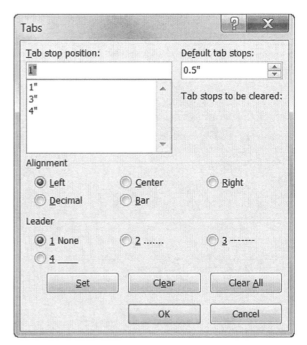

You can control what characters are inserted in the otherwise blank area created by the tab. These characters are called **leaders**, and are controlled with the Tabs command from the Format menu. Leaders are often used with right-aligned tabs or decimal tabs, particularly when the text column is quite wide and the tab will cover a wide area.

Set a few tab stops by using the instructions and practice file below.

You will need to access practice files in your course online for this lesson. We've placed instructions in the appendix of this book on pages 198-199.

I. **TRUE/FALSE.**
   Mark the following true or false.

1. To set a tab stop, select the alignment and choose the type of leader and the location of the tab stop on the ruler.
   - ● true
   - ○ false

2. You need to press the TAB key twice to make the insertion point move to the next tab stop.
   - ○ true
   - ● false

3. The Tabs dialog box is slower, but more accurate than setting tabs with the ruler.
   - ● true
   - ○ false

4. The center tab is the default and most common type of tab.
   - ○ true
   - ● false

Adjusting and Removing Tab Stops

Tab stops are also easy to adjust and remove.

Adjust a tab stop with the ruler

Click and drag the tab stop to the desired position on the ruler. The tab stop is moved.

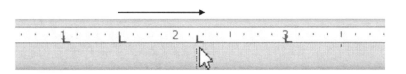

Moving a left tab stop.

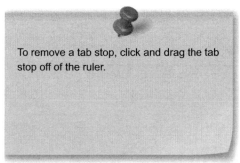

To remove a tab stop, click and drag the tab stop off of the ruler.

Adjust a tab stop with the Tabs dialog box

1. Click the Home tab on the Ribbon and click the Dialog Box Launcher in the Paragraph group. The Paragraph dialog box appears.

2. Click the Tabs button near the bottom of the Paragraph dialog box.

3. Select the tab stop you want to adjust.

4. Make the adjustments in the dialog box and click Set.

5. Click OK to confirm the change. The tab stop is moved. If you selected text that used the tab stop, the text adjusts to the new position of the tab stop.

Tip: If you selected text that used the tab stop, the text adjusts to the new position of the tab stop.

Adjust a tab leader

One setting that isn't available on the ruler is tab leaders. A tab leader is a line from the current location to the next tab stop. Tab leaders are usually found in tables of contents and menus.

1. Open the Tabs dialog box.

2. Select the tab stop to which you want to add a leader from the Tab stop position list.

3. Select a leader option. There are four leader options listed under the Leader section.

4. Click Set. You can continue to add tab leaders to other tabs until you are finished.

5. Click OK.

Change........ % Change	
Right............Decimal	
$968,723...................	+32.38%
$747,295....................	+6.151%
$529,207...................	+13.8%

Now that you've set some tab stops, let's try adjusting and moving them.

You will need to access practice files in your course online for this lesson. We've placed instructions in the appendix of this book on page 200.

If you have access to Microsoft Office, have you tried these tasks in the software? Practicing will help you better comprehend and remember how to apply the skills you're learning.

When you feel comfortable completing these tasks without referring to the listed steps, you're ready to move on with your training.

Using Left and Right Indents

Indenting adds blank space between the page margin and the paragraph text. Long quotations, lists, and bibliographies are a few examples of paragraphs that are often indented.

Left indent

The most common type of indent is a left indent, in which text is moved away from the left margin.

1. Select or place the insertion point in the paragraph(s) you want to change.

2. Click the Home tab on the Ribbon and click the Increase Indent button in the Paragraph group. The paragraph(s) are indented 0.5", or to the next indent level in the document. Another way to increase an indent is to click and drag the Left Indent marker on the ruler. Or, click the Dialog Box Launcher in the Paragraph group and enter how much space you want the paragraph indented by in the Left indentation box. Or, click the Page Layout tab on the Ribbon and adjust the Indent Left box in the Paragraph group.

To use the left or right indent markers, the ruler must be displayed. To show the ruler, click the View tab on the Ribbon and click the Ruler check box in the Show/Hide group.

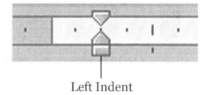

Left Indent

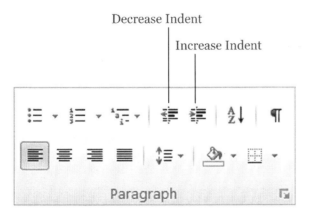

Decrease Indent

Increase Indent

Paragraph

Right indent

A right indentation of a paragraph moves text away from the right margin.

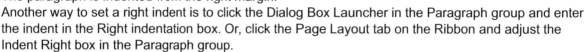
Right Indent

1. Select or place the insertion point in the paragraph(s) you want to change.

2. Click and drag the Right Indent marker on the ruler. The paragraph is indented from the right margin.
Another way to set a right indent is to click the Dialog Box Launcher in the Paragraph group and enter the indent in the Right indentation box. Or, click the Page Layout tab on the Ribbon and adjust the Indent Right box in the Paragraph group.

Practice using left and right indents on the file below.

You will need to access practice files in your course online for this lesson. We've placed instructions in the appendix of this book on page 201.

Using Hanging and First Line Indents

Besides the left and right indents, two special indents can be used in your paragraphs: hanging and first line indents.

First line indent

A first line indentation lets you indent the first line of a paragraph independently of the other lines. Many people do this with a tab instead of changing the indent settings.

Hanging Indent   First Line Indent
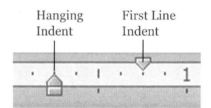

1. Select or position the insertion point in the paragraph(s) you want to indent.

2. Click the Home tab on the Ribbon and click the Dialog Box Launcher in the Paragraph group.

3. Click the Special list arrow in the Indentation section and select First line.

4. Enter the desired indent amount in the By box, and click OK. You can also click and drag the First Line indent marker on the ruler. Or, click the tab alignment box until you see the First Line Indent marker, then click where you want to insert the indent on the ruler.

Hanging indent

In hanging indentation, the first line of a paragraph stays put next to the left margin while the other lines in the paragraph are indented. Hanging indentations are often used in bibliographies or lists.

1. Select or position the insertion point in the paragraph(s) you want to indent.

2. Click the Home tab on the Ribbon and click the Dialog Box Launcher in the Paragraph group.

3. Click the Special list arrow in the Indentation section and select Hanging.

4. Enter the desired indent amount in the By box, and click OK. You can also click and drag the hanging indent marker on the ruler. Or, click the tab alignment box until you see the Hanging indent marker, then click where you want to insert the indent on the ruler.

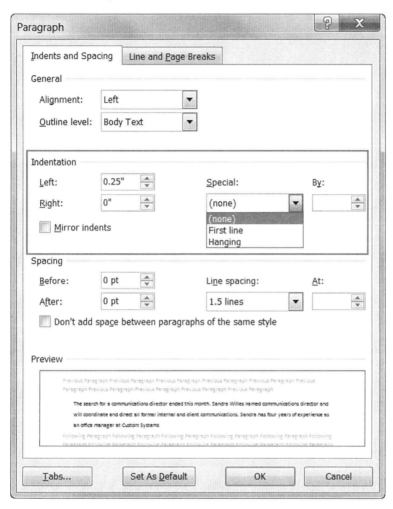

Let's practice using hanging and first line indents! The instructions below will teach you how.

You will need to access practice files in your course online for this lesson. We've placed instructions in the appendix of this book on page 202.

I. MATCHING.
Match the phrases below to the correct type of indentation.

1. _A_ the first line of a paragraph stays put next to the left margin

2. _B_ lets you indent the first line of a paragraph independently of the other lines

3. _A_ all lines other than the first line of the paragraph are indented

4. _A_ often used in bibliographies or lists

5. _B_ can be made using a tab instead of changing the indent settings

A. hanging indent

B. first line indent

1. How to play DVD
2. NOT-
3.
4
5. Open paragraph dialog box, click special list row, select hanging & specify an amount in the Box

1. F
2. F
3. T
4. F

Unit 6
Formatting the Page

Formatting the Page – Introduction

Instead of working with characters and paragraphs, this unit takes a step back and looks at how to change the appearance of entire pages. When you format a page, you determine the margins between the text and the edge of the page, the orientation of the page, and the size of the paper. These topics are covered in this unit. We will also explain how to add a header or footer that appears at the top or bottom of every page in your document, how to control where the page breaks, and how to use multiple page formats.

Adjusting Margins

A margin is the empty space between a document's contents and the edges of the page. Word's default margins are 1 inch on each side of the page, but you can easily change the margins to accommodate the needs of your document.

1. Click the Page Layout tab on the Ribbon and click the Margins button in the Page Setup group. A list of common page margins appears. Another way to adjust margins is to click the Margins button in the Page Setup group and select Custom Margins. Then change the document's margins on the Margins tab of the Page Setup dialog box. Or, click and drag the Left Margin, Right Margin, Top Margin, or Bottom Margin line on the ruler.
2. Select a margin setting.
3. Click OK. The margin setting will be applied to the document.

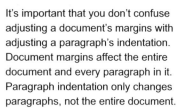

Highlights

It's important that you don't confuse adjusting a document's margins with adjusting a paragraph's indentation. Document margins affect the entire document and every paragraph in it. Paragraph indentation only changes paragraphs, not the entire document.

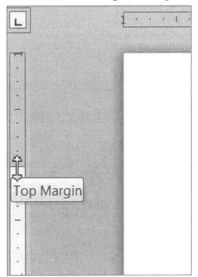

Top Margin

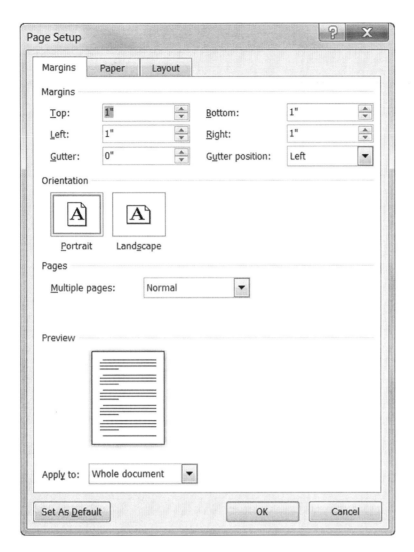

Tip: If you intend to bind a document and require extra space for the bindings, use the Gutter setting on the Margins tab in the Page Setup dialog box. The gutter margin is to designate an additional margin added to a page layout to compensate for the part of the paper made unusable by the binding process. In single-sheet layouts, the gutter margin is typically the area where you might three-hole punch your paper.

You will need to access practice files in your course online for this lesson. We've placed instructions in the appendix of this book on page 203.

Changing Page Orientation and Size

The page orientation and size are two of the most obvious page layout properties of a document.

Page orientation

Every document you print uses one of two different types of page orientations: Portrait and Landscape.

1. Click the Page Layout tab on the Ribbon and click the Orientation button in the Page Setup group. A list of two options will appear:

    Portrait: In Portrait orientation, the paper is taller than it is wide—like a portrait painting.

Landscape: In Landscape orientation, the paper is wider than it is tall—like a landscape painting.

2. Select the page orientation you want to use. The page layout will change accordingly. If the Ruler is displayed, notice that the dimensions of the page have changed. For example, if you were using an 8.5" x 11" page, the horizontal part of the ruler is now 11 inches across, rather than 8.5". You can also click the Dialog Box Launcher in the Page Setup Group. On the Margins tab, click the orientation you want to use.

Tip: Here's an easy way to remember the difference between Page Layout options: Think of a landscaped backyard against the horizon. This will help you remember that Landscape orientation is horizontal, and Portrait orientation is vertical.

Page size

People normally print on standard Letter-sized (8½ x 11) paper, but Word can also print on other paper sizes, such as Legal-sized (8½ x 14) and other custom-sized paper. This means that you can use Word not only to print letters, but also postcards, tickets, flyers, and any other documents that use a non-standard paper size.

Highlights

If the size you want to use doesn't appear in the list, select More Paper Sizes. The Paper tab of the Page Setup dialog box appears, where there are more page size options, and where you can enter a custom paper size if you wish.

1. Click the Page Layout tab on the Ribbon and click the Size button in the Page Setup group. A list of common page sizes will appear.

2. Select the page size you want to use. The document on the screen will adjust to the selected size.

Go ahead and try changing page orientation and size using the instructions below.

You will need to access practice files in your course online for this lesson. We've placed instructions in the appendix of this book on page 204.

I. MULTIPLE CHOICE.
Choose the best answer.

1. If the page size you want doesn't appear in the list, select (◯Page Layout, ◉More Paper Sizes).

2. The standard Letter-sized paper is (◯8 1/2 x 14, ◉8 1/2 x 11).

3. In Landscape orientation, the page is (◉horizontal, ◯vertical).

4. Clicking the Dialog Box Launcher, the Margins tab, and then Portrait or Landscape is one way to change (◯page size, ◉page orientation).

Using Columns

Newsletters and magazines often arrange text in two or more columns.

Format columns

1. Click the Page Layout tab on the Ribbon and click the Columns button in the Page Setup group. A list of popular column layouts will appear.
2. Select the column arrangement you want to use. The document on the screen will adjust to the selected layout.

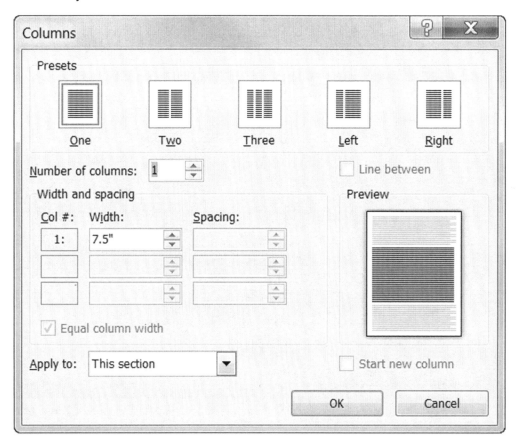

Use a column break

When you insert a column break, the insertion point jumps to the beginning of the next column on the page. For example, if you wanted to leave a column empty halfway down the page to leave space for a pull quote or picture, inserting a column break would allow you to continue your text in the next column.

1. Click the Page Layout tab on the Ribbon and click the Breaks button in the Page Setup group. A list of available breaks will appear.

2. Select Column from the list. The column break will be inserted and the insertion point will move to the beginning of the next column.

With the help of the instructions below practice using columns.

> You will need to access practice files in your course online for this lesson. We've placed instructions in the appendix of this book on page 205.

Using Page Breaks

This lesson explains how to control where the page breaks in a document. You may want to have the Show Characters feature turned on so that you can see where the breaks appear. To do this, click the Home tab on the Ribbon and click the Show/Hide button in the Paragraph group. To turn off special characters, click this button again.

Start a new page

1. Place the insertion point where you want to begin a new page.

2. Click the Insert tab on the Ribbon and click the Page Break button in the Pages group. Word will insert a page break at the insertion point, and any page contents that appear after the insertion point will appear on the new page. Another way to insert a page break is to press CTRL + ENTER. You can also click the Page Layout tab on the Ribbon and click the Breaks button in the Page Setup group. Select Page Break from the list.

Section Breaks

Next Page
Insert a section break and start the new section on the next page.

Continuous
Insert a section break and start the new section on the same page.

Even Page
Insert a section break and start the new section on the next even-numbered page.

Odd Page
Insert a section break and start the new section on the next odd-numbered page.

Insert a blank page

Use this command to insert a blank page anywhere in a document.

1. Click the Insert tab on the Ribbon and click the Blank Page button in the Pages group.

2. Word inserts a blank page at the insertion point. The blank page is really just two page breaks.

> To remove a page break, view the document in Draft view, select the page break, and press DELETE.

Use paragraph line and page breaks

You can also control pagination with paragraph formatting. For example, you can make sure paragraphs appear on the same page without being on separate pages, or make sure a paragraph always starts on a new page.

1. Select the paragraph(s) to which you want to add pagination formatting.

2. Click the Page Layout tab on the Ribbon and click the Dialog Box Launcher in the Paragraph group. The Paragraph dialog box will appear.

3. Click the Line and Page Breaks tab and select the pagination and formatting options you want to use. When you're finished, click OK. The formatting options will apply to the selected paragraph(s).

Paragraph Line and Page Break Options	
Widow/Orphan control	Prevents Word from printing the last line of a paragraph by itself at the top of a page (widow) or the first line of a paragraph by itself at the bottom of a page (orphan). This option is selected by default.
Keep with next	Prevents the page from breaking between the selected paragraph and the following paragraph.
Keep lines together	Prevents the page from breaking within a paragraph.
Page break before	Inserts a page break before the selected paragraph. This is a good option for major headings.
Suppress line numbers	This prevents line numbers from appearing next to selected paragraphs if the Line Numbering option is on. This setting has no effect in documents or sections with no line numbers.
Don't hyphenate	Excludes a paragraph from automatic hyphenation.

Take a minute to practice inserting page breaks in a document.

You will need to access practice files in your course online for this lesson. We've placed instructions in the appendix of this book on page 206.

I. MATCHING.
Match the correct term to the definition.

1. _B_ the last line of a paragraph by itself at the top of a page

2. _E_ inserts a page break before the selected paragraph

3. _C_ excludes a paragraph from automatic hyphenation

4. _D_ prevents the page from breaking within a paragraph

5. _A_ the first line of a paragraph by itself at the bottom of a page

6. _F_ prevents line numbers from appearing next to selected paragraphs

A. widow
B. orphan
C. don't hyphenate
D. keep lines together
E. page break before
F. suppress line numbers

Working with Section Breaks

Section breaks can help you control where pages break in the document, but they also allow you to apply different page formatting in the same document. A section break allows you to use different page layouts—such as margins, page orientation, headers and footers, columns, and sequence of page numbers—in the same document.

1. Click the Page Layout tab on the Ribbon and click the Breaks button in the Page Setup group. A list of the breaks you can insert in the document appears.

2. Select the type of break you want to insert. The break will be inserted into the document.

Tip: To remove a break, select the break and press DELETE.

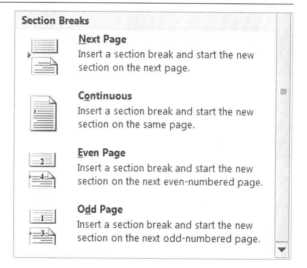

Section Breaks

Next Page
Insert a section break and start the new section on the next page.

Continuous
Insert a section break and start the new section on the same page.

Even Page
Insert a section break and start the new section on the next even-numbered page.

Odd Page
Insert a section break and start the new section on the next odd-numbered page.

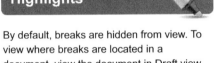

Highlights

By default, breaks are hidden from view. To view where breaks are located in a document, view the document in Draft view. Or, click the Home tab and click the Show/Hide All button in the Paragraph group to view breaks in Print Layout view.

Types of Section Breaks

Next Page Section Break	Inserts a section break at the insertion point and inserts a page break so the new section starts at the beginning of a new page.
Continuous Section Break	Inserts a section break at the insertion point and starts the section immediately, without inserting a page break.
Even Page Section Break	Inserts a section break at the insertion point and starts the next section on the next even-numbered page. If the section break falls on an even-numbered page, Word leaves the next odd-numbered page blank.
Odd Page Section Break	Inserts a section break at the insertion point and starts the next section on the next odd-numbered page. If the section break falls on an odd-numbered page, Word leaves the next even-numbered page blank.

Practice working with page breaks by using the instructions and practice file below.

You will need to access practice files in your course online for this lesson. We've placed instructions in the appendix of this book on page 207.

Working with Line Numbers

Adding line numbers to documents is the most direct way to guide users through complex and lengthy documents. When you apply line numbers in Word, the numbers are displayed in the left margin of the document. If there are columns in the document, the numbers appear to the left of each newspaper-style column. Line numbers are especially useful when you need to refer to a specific line in a document, such as a script or a legal document. You should also know that while each line in a document can be numbered, lines from inserted objects such as tables, footnotes, endnotes, text boxes, frames, headers, and footers are not included in line numbering. In addition, line numbers are only visible in Print Layout view and Print Preview.

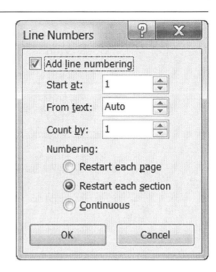

1. Click the Page Layout tab on the Ribbon and click the Line Numbers button in the Page Setup group. A list of ways you can add line numbers will appear:

   None: Removes line numbering in the document.

   Continuous: Adds continuous line numbering to each section of the document.

   Restart Each Page: Adds line numbering to the current page of the document. Restarts numbering at the beginning of the next page.

   Restart Each Section: Adds line numbering to the current section of the document. Restarts numbering at the beginning of any added sections.

   Suppress for Current Section: Removes line numbering for the current section.

2. Select a line numbering option. The line numbers are applied to the document.

1   Excel

2   # 2...4...6...8 everyone consolidate

3   *Combining data ranges from multiple worksheets*

4   These days, you can consolidate your credit card debt, your student loans, or your company's

5   subsidiaries. But did you know that you can also consolidate data from multiple Excel worksheets? For

6   example, if you have sales data from three different offices on three different worksheets, Excel can

7   total them for you on another worksheet.

8   **Three ways to consolidate**

9   Excel provides three ways to consolidate information: by position, by category, or by using 3-D

10   references.

11   • Consolidating by position is the most restrictive. To use this approach, data in all the worksheets must

12   be arranged in exactly the same order and location.

13   • Consolidating by category is slightly less restrictive—all the worksheets need to have the same row

14   and column labels in order to be consolidated, but the data can be arranged differently. Excel uses the

15   labels to match the data.

16   • Consolidating using 3-D references is the least restrictive method. You can create formulas to

17   consolidate data that is arranged in any fashion, and the consolidation updates automatically when the

18   source data changes.

19   Using either of the first two methods, you can consolidate manually or set it up to update automatically

20   when the source data changes, but you can't change which cell ranges are included in the consolidation.

21   Now let's look at each of the methods in more detail.

22   **Consolidating by position**

23   *When to use:* If data is laid out in identical cells in all consolidating worksheets.

24   Before you consolidate by position, make sure that the data is arranged in labeled rows and

25   columns without blank rows or columns. Each of the ranges you want to consolidate needs to be on a

26   separate worksheet, with a blank worksheet used for the consolidation's destination. Each range needs

27   to be laid out the same because you're going to be combining data from the same cell in each of the

28   ranges.

Tip: If you are applying numbering to a document that has several sections, select the sections to which you want to add numbering first.

Highlights

To control line numbering options through the Line Numbers dialog box, select Line Numbering from the Line Numbers button list. Click the Line Numbers button and select the line numbering options you want to use from the Line Numbers dialog box.

Ready to try working with line numbers? Use the files below to practice!

You will need to access practice files in your course online for this lesson. We've placed instructions in the appendix of this book on page 208.

Working with Hyphenation

Word can automatically hyphenate your text so that rather than pushing a long word at the end of the line to the next line, it breaks across lines with a hyphen. This is especially useful in documents where a lot of text has to appear in a small amount of space, such as when using justified paragraph alignment in columns, for example.

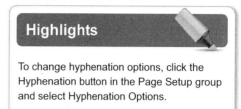

Highlights

To change hyphenation options, click the Hyphenation button in the Page Setup group and select Hyphenation Options.

1. Click the Page Layout tab on the Ribbon and click the Hyphenation button in the Page Setup group. Hyphenation is turned off by default, but you may turn on automatic or manual hyphenation:

   Automatic: Word automatically inserts hyphens where they are needed, according to the hyphenation zone. If the document is edited and lines change, Word re-hyphenates the document.

   Manual: Word searches the text for words to hyphenate and asks if you would like to insert an optional hyphen. Word does not re-hyphenate the document for you. If you choose to manually hyphenate, Word will ask for approval before it inserts a hyphen.

2. Choose how you want to hyphenate the document. Word begins the hyphenation process using the method you chose.

3. To remove hyphenation, click the Hyphenation button in the Page Setup group and select None.

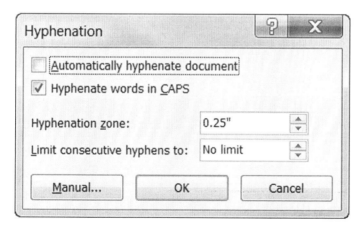

Let's try working with hyphenation using the files below.

You will need to access practice files in your course online for this lesson. We've placed instructions in the appendix of this book on page 209.

Working with the Page Background

Dress up pages in a document with page borders and background settings. You can line the margins of your pages with borders to give them finished edges or to bring out certain pages, and you can even create your own page designs using colors and watermarks.

Page with color, border, and watermark applied.

Add page borders

You can line the margins of your pages with borders to give them finished edges or to bring out certain pages.

1. Click the Page Layout tab on the Ribbon and click the Page Borders button in the Page Background group. The Page Border tab of the Borders and Shading dialog box appears.

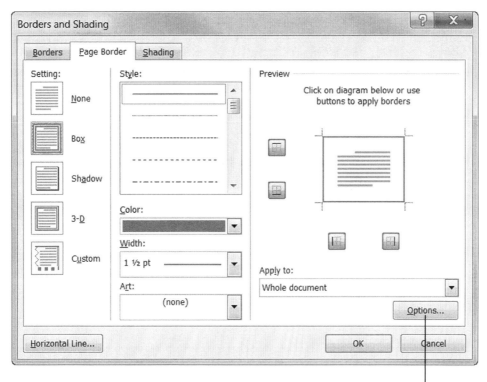

Click the Options button to define how far
away from margins you want the border

2. Choose border properties, such as style, color, width, or art. These properties change how the border(s) will appear around the page.

3. Click the side(s) (top, bottom, left, and/or right) of the page in the Preview diagram where you want to apply the borders. When the preview area looks the way you want the borders to look, you're ready to apply the borders.

> **Whole document:** Applies the borders to all pages in the document.
>
> **This section:** Applies borders only to the current section.
>
> **This section – First page only:** Applies borders to the first page of the current section and nowhere else.
>
> **This section – All except first page:** Applies borders to all pages in the current section, except the first page.

4. Click OK. The borders will apply to the page(s) in the document.

Tip: You may also use the Setting options along the left side of the Page Border tab to apply borders.

Add page color

Add color to the background of one or several pages in the document. This formatting feature is only visible in electronic copies of the document: Word will not print the page color.

1. Click the Page Layout tab on the Ribbon and click the Page Color button in the Page Background group. The Page Color button displays the ten colors in the current color theme, and five shades of each color. This makes it easy to have a consistent look and feel in the document.

2. Select a color from the list. The color is applied to the page. To remove page color, click the Page Color button and select No Color.

Add a watermark

A watermark is discrete text that indicates a document should be specially treated. It does not obscure text on the page.

1. Click the Page Layout tab on the Ribbon and click the Watermark button in the Page Background group. A list of built-in watermarks will appear, organized in different categories: Confidential, Disclaimers, Urgent. A preview of how watermarks appear on the page is shown next to each list option.
2. Select the watermark you would like to use. The watermark will apply to the pages of the document. To remove the watermark, click the Watermark button and select Remove Watermark.

Now you're ready to take on the challenge of working with page backgrounds! Use the instructions below to try your hand.

You will need to access practice files in your course online for this lesson. We've placed instructions in the appendix of this book on page 210.

I. **FILL IN THE BLANK.**
Enter the correct word in the blank provided.

1. When you color the background of a document, you are adding _page color_.

2. In the "Apply to" list, _This Section_ will apply borders only to the current section.

3. A _watermark_ is the discrete text you can add to a page that does not obscure the text.

This section
borders
Setting
page color
watermark

4. You can line the margins of your pages with *borders* to give them a finished edge look.

5. Another way to apply borders is to use the *settings* options along the left side of the Page Border tab.

Adding a Cover Page and Page Numbers

A cover page and page numbers are two things that are easy to add and that make your document look polished and professional.

Cover page

A cover page for your document is like the cover of a book: it contains basic information, such as the title of the document, date, and author, presented in a way that is eye-catching and welcoming to the reader.

1. Click the Insert tab on the Ribbon and click the Cover Page button in the Pages group. A list of built-in cover pages will appear. Notice that each design has a name, which makes it easier to match up with other built-in elements, such as built-in headers and footers.

2. Select the cover page you want to insert in the document. The cover page always appears as the first page in the document, no matter where the insertion point is located when it is inserted. When inserted, placeholders for information appear on the cover page. Word tries to insert as much information as it can, such as user information like your name and company name, but you will probably have to insert information manually as well.

3. Click in a placeholder and type your own text.

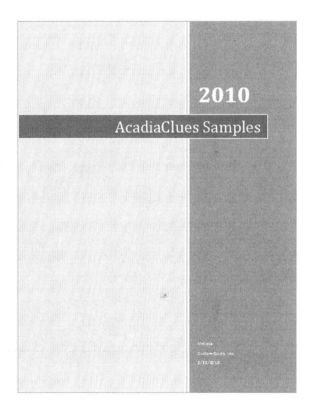

Page numbers

Adding page numbers is easier than ever in Word 2010, and it adds a lot to documents, especially really long ones.

1. Click the Insert tab on the Ribbon and click the Page Number button in the Header & Footer group. First, choose where you would like the numbers to appear on the page. You can include the page numbers in three different places on the page—top, bottom, and margins.

2. Select where you want the page numbers to appear. A list of the available built-in page number styles appears.

3. Select the page number style you want to use. The page number style you chose appears on the current page and all the other pages in the document.

Tip: To remove page numbers, click the Page Number button and select Remove Page Numbers.

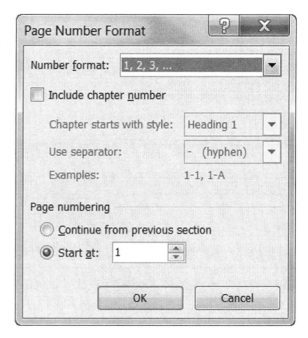

Highlights

If you like one of the built-in options but want the numbers to appear a little differently, you can change the number format. To modify page numbers, click the Page Number button and select Format Page Numbers. Select the style of number you want to use from the Page Number Format dialog box.

Try adding a cover and page numbers to a document using the files below.

You will need to access practice files in your course online for this lesson. We've placed instructions in the appendix of this book on page 211.

I. TRUE/FALSE.
Mark the following true or false.

1. To add page numbers, click the Insert tab, click the Page Number button, select where you want the page numbers to appear, and then select the number style you want to use.
   - ● true
   - ○ false

2. A cover page helps organize where each page of the document will be, especially in long documents.
   - ○ true
   - ● false

3. Not every design in the built-in cover pages has a name.

   ○ true

   Ø false

4. To remove page numbers, click the Page Number button and select Remove Page Numbers.

   Ø true

   ○ false

Using Headers and Footers

Documents with several pages often have information—such as the page number, the document's title, or the date—located at the top or bottom of every page. Text that appears at the top of every page in a document is called a header, while text appearing at the bottom of each page is called a footer.

Insert a built-in header or footer

Built-in headers and footers can be modified to suit the needs of your document or project. Let's look first at how to get them onto a page in the first place.

1. Click the Insert tab on the Ribbon and click the Header or Footer button in the Header & Footer group. A list of built-in options appears. Each option looks different and contains different attributes. For example, some include placeholders for the title and date, while others include cross-references to styles within the document.
2. Select a built-in option to use as a document header or footer. The header or footer is added to the document.

Tip: Point to a built-in header or footer option to view its attributes and a description of how it might be used best.

Create a header or footer

You don't have to use one of Word's built-in headers or footers: you can create one of your own.

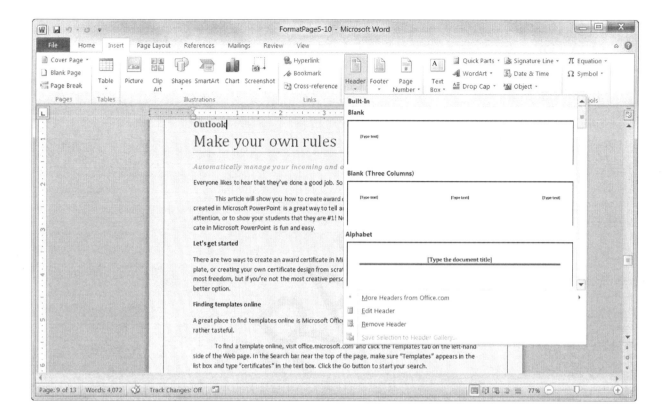

1. Click the Insert tab on the Ribbon and click the Header or Footer button in the Header & Footer group.

2. Select Edit Header or Edit Footer from the list. The Header & Footer Design tab appears on the Ribbon. Use these commands to work with and insert elements into your headers and footers.

3. Position the insertion point where you want to insert the text or element. The header and footer areas have the same formatting abilities as the main area of the document. You can use the commands in the Position group to help align and position the contents of the header or footer.

4. Enter text and/or insert objects using the Insert group of the Design tab under Header & Footer Tools. When the header or footer looks the way you want it to, close Header and Footer view to resume work on the rest of the document

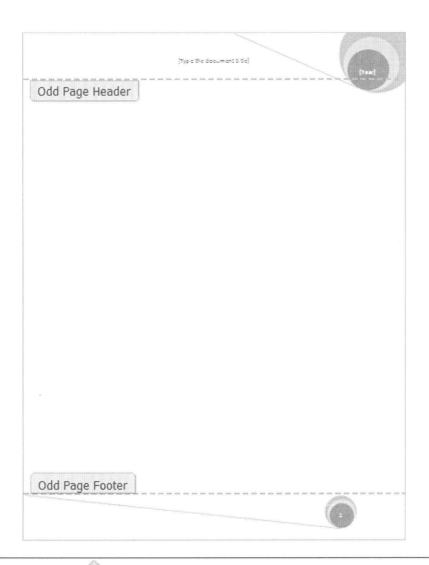

[Type the document title]

[Year]

Odd Page Header

Odd Page Footer

Highlights

Changes made to the header or footer on a page will change the other headers and footers in that section. Use a document with section breaks to have different headers and footers within the document.

Use different headers and footers on odd and even pages

Some built-in headers and footers were made to appear on odd or even pages. To use these headers and footers correctly, or to create your own odd and even-page headers and footers, you must change the page layout. When this option is selected, the odd and even pages work independently. So, you must insert a header for the odd pages, and a header for the even pages: one header won't work for both.

1. Click the Insert tab on the Ribbon and click the Header or Footer button in the Header & Footer group.

2. Select Edit Header or Edit Footer from the list. The Design tab will appear on the Ribbon under Header & Footer Tools.

3. Click the Different Odd & Even Pages check box in the Options group.

    Another way to apply different headers and footers to odd and even pages is to click the Page Layout tab on the Ribbon and click the Dialog Box Launcher in the Page Setup group. Click the Layout tab and make sure the Different odd and even check box is checked.

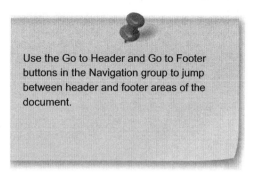

Use the Go to Header and Go to Footer buttons in the Navigation group to jump between header and footer areas of the document.

4. Insert a header or footer on an odd page. Then insert a header or footer on an even page. When you insert the headers and footers, they are formatted differently on the odd and even pages.

Odd Page Footer
[Pick the date]

Even Page Footer
[Pick the date]

Header and Footer Design tab Groups	
Header & Footer	Apply built-in header, footer, and page number options.
Insert	Insert Date & Time, a Picture or Clip Art, or a Quick Part field.
Navigation	Switch between headers and footers and jump to other sections.
Options	Apply a different header or footer to the first page in a section, different odd & even pages, and choose to show document text.
Position	Choose how far away from the margins you want the headers and footers to appear, and control header and footer alignment.

Be sure to get some practice working with headers and footers.

You will need to access practice files in your course online for this lesson. We've placed instructions in the appendix of this book on page 212.

Unit 7

Working with Themes and Styles

Working with Themes and Styles – Introduction

This unit covers formatting features that can save you tons of time as you create and format documents.

First, we'll learn all about styles. A style is a set of character and paragraph formats stored under a name. Styles are useful because you can apply a whole group of formatting options in a single step. If you decide to change the formatting options of a style, every character or paragraph formatted with that style is automatically updated with the new formatting options, instead of having to go through the document and manually update each and every paragraph. Styles are rather abstract, so don't worry if you still don't understand them—they will make more sense after you work with them.

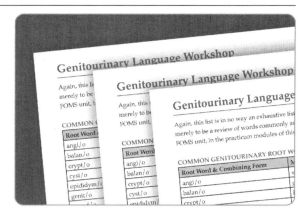

The final lessons in the unit talk about document themes, a great way to make your documents look cohesive and professionally designed.

Applying a Style

Microsoft recognizes that styles are efficient and useful in creating a document, so they have created sets of coordinating styles that have all the styles you need to build a document. In previous versions, users were left to create most of their own styles from scratch. Now, styles are very accessible with a wide range of them prominently displayed on the Ribbon.

A **style** is a group of format settings stored under a single name. Quick Styles are sets of styles that are designed to work together to create attractive and professional looking documents.

Each set of quick styles includes all the styles you need to build a document. For example, you can apply the "Quote" style if you are quoting something in a document, or the "Title" style for the document's main heading. Using quick styles rather than your own formatting has several advantages:

- The document looks professional and is easy to read.
- Styles provide consistency and can apply several formatting properties at one time.
- If you change the formatting properties of a style, all instances of the style are updated with the formatting changes.

Apply a style

Choose a style that is appropriate for the text, and then apply the style.

1. Select the text to which you want to apply the style.

2. Click the Home tab on the Ribbon and click the style you want to use in the Styles Gallery in the Styles group. The style will be applied to the document. To view all the styles in the quick style set at the same time, click the More button to expand the group.

Tip: If the style that you want does not appear in the Styles Gallery, press CTRL + SHIFT + S to open the Apply Styles task pane. Under Style Name, type the name of the style you want to use.

Click a style in the Style Gallery to apply it to text. The current style is highlighted.

Click the Change Styles button to select a different quick style set.

Use these buttons to view other styles in the quick style set.

As you point to different styles in the Style Set list, the document changes to show you how it will look with the style set.

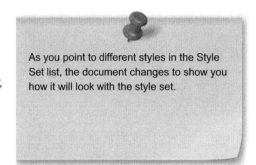

Apply a different Quick Style Set

Word's built-in style sets are professionally designed to convey a certain tone. Want your document to look more formal? Use the Formal style set, and the styles will take on formatting properties that make text look more formal.

1. Click the Home tab on the Ribbon and click the Change Styles button in the Styles group.

2. Point to Style Set and select the style set you want to use. The styles available in the Styles Gallery change to reflect the style set you selected.

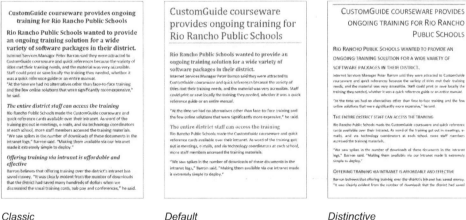

Classic   *Default*   *Distinctive*

Elegant

CUSTOMGUIDE COURSEWARE PROVIDES ONGOING TRAINING FOR RIO RANCHO PUBLIC SCHOOLS

RIO RANCHO PUBLIC SCHOOLS WANTED TO PROVIDE AN ONGOING TRAINING SOLUTION FOR A WIDE VARIETY OF SOFTWARE PACKAGES IN THEIR DISTRICT.

Internet Services Manager Peter Barron said they were attracted to CustomGuide courseware and quick references because the variety of titles met their training needs, and the material was very accessible. Staff could print or save locally the training they needed, whether it was a quick reference guide or an entire manual.

"At the time we had no alternatives other than face-to-face training and the few online solutions that were significantly more expensive," he said.

Fancy

CustomGuide courseware provides ongoing training for Rio Rancho Public Schools

Rio Rancho Public Schools wanted to provide an ongoing training solution for a wide variety of software packages in their district.

Internet Services Manager Peter Barron said they were attracted to CustomGuide courseware and quick references because the variety of titles met their training needs, and the material was very accessible. Staff could print or save locally the training they needed, whether it was a quick reference guide or an entire manual.

"At the time we had no alternatives other than face-to-face training and the few online solutions that were significantly more expensive," he said.

The entire district staff can access the training

Rio Rancho Public Schools made the CustomGuide courseware and quick reference cards available over their intranet. As word of the training got out in meetings, e-mails, and via technology coordinators at each school, more staff members accessed the training materials.

"We saw spikes in the number of downloads of these documents in the intranet logs," Barron said. "Making them available via our intranet made it extremely simple to deploy."

Offering training via intranet is affordable and effective

Barron believes that offering training over the district's intranet has saved money. "It was clearly evident from the number of downloads that the district had saved many hundreds of dollars when we discounted the usual training costs, sub pay and conferences," he said.

Formal

CUSTOMGUIDE COURSEWARE PROVIDES ONGOING TRAINING FOR RIO RANCHO PUBLIC SCHOOLS

RIO RANCHO PUBLIC SCHOOLS WANTED TO PROVIDE AN ONGOING TRAINING SOLUTION FOR A WIDE VARIETY OF SOFTWARE PACKAGES IN THEIR DISTRICT.

Internet Services Manager Peter Barron said they were attracted to CustomGuide courseware and quick references because the variety of titles met their training needs, and the material was very accessible. Staff could print or save locally the training they needed, whether it was a quick reference guide or an entire manual.

"At the time we had no alternatives other than face-to-face training and the few online solutions that were significantly more expensive," he said.

THE ENTIRE DISTRICT STAFF CAN ACCESS THE TRAINING

Rio Rancho Public Schools made the CustomGuide courseware and quick reference cards available over their intranet. As word of the training got out in meetings, e-mails, and via technology coordinators at each school, more staff members accessed the training materials.

Manuscript

CustomGuide courseware provides ongoing training for Rio Rancho Public Schools

Rio Rancho Public Schools wanted to provide an ongoing training solution for a wide variety of software packages in their district.

Internet Services Manager Peter Barron said they were attracted to CustomGuide courseware and quick references because the variety of titles met their training needs, and the material was very accessible. Staff could print or save locally the training they needed, whether it was a quick reference guide or an entire manual.

Modern

CUSTOMGUIDE COURSEWARE PROVIDES ONGOING TRAINING FOR RIO RANCHO PUBLIC SCHOOLS

RIO RANCHO PUBLIC SCHOOLS WANTED TO PROVIDE AN ONGOING TRAINING SOLUTION FOR A WIDE VARIETY OF SOFTWARE PACKAGES IN THEIR DISTRICT.

Internet Services Manager Peter Barron said they were attracted to CustomGuide courseware and quick references because the variety of titles met their training needs, and the material was very accessible. Staff could print or save locally the training they needed, whether it was a quick reference guide or an entire manual.

"At the time we had no alternatives other than face-to-face training and the few online solutions that were significantly more expensive," he said.

THE ENTIRE DISTRICT STAFF CAN ACCESS THE TRAINING

Rio Rancho Public Schools made the CustomGuide courseware and quick reference cards available over their intranet. As word of the training got out in meetings, e-mails, and via technology coordinators at each school, more staff members accessed the training materials.

"We saw spikes in the number of downloads of these documents in the intranet logs," Barron said. "Making them available via our intranet made it extremely simple to deploy."

Simple

CUSTOMGUIDE COURSEWARE PROVIDES ONGOING TRAINING FOR RIO RANCHO PUBLIC SCHOOLS

RIO RANCHO PUBLIC SCHOOLS WANTED TO PROVIDE AN ONGOING TRAINING SOLUTION FOR A WIDE VARIETY OF SOFTWARE PACKAGES IN THEIR DISTRICT.

Internet Services Manager Peter Barron said they were attracted to CustomGuide courseware and quick references because the variety of titles met their training needs, and the material was very accessible. Staff could print or save locally the training they needed, whether it was a quick reference guide or an entire manual.

"At the time we had no alternatives other than face-to-face training and the few online solutions that were significantly more expensive," he said.

THE ENTIRE DISTRICT STAFF CAN ACCESS THE TRAINING

Rio Rancho Public Schools made the CustomGuide courseware and quick reference cards available over their intranet. As word of the training got out in meetings, e-mails, and via technology coordinators at each school, more staff members accessed the training materials.

"We saw spikes in the number of downloads of these documents in the intranet logs," Barron said. "Making them available via our intranet made it extremely simple to deploy."

Traditional

CustomGuide courseware provides ongoing training for Rio Rancho Public Schools

Rio Rancho Public Schools wanted to provide an ongoing training solution for a wide variety of software packages in their district.

Internet Services Manager Peter Barron said they were attracted to CustomGuide courseware and quick references because the variety of titles met their training needs, and the material was very accessible. Staff could print or save locally the training they needed, whether it was a quick reference guide or an entire manual.

"At the time we had no alternatives other than face-to-face training and the few online solutions that were significantly more expensive," he said.

The entire district staff can access the training

Rio Rancho Public Schools made the CustomGuide courseware and quick reference cards available over their intranet. As word of the training got out in meetings, e-mails, and via technology coordinators at each school, more staff members accessed the training materials.

"We saw spikes in the number of downloads of these documents in the intranet logs," Barron said. "Making them available via our intranet made it extremely simple to deploy."

Highlights

In most cases, choosing a different quick style set does not change the font type or the font theme being used; it just applies different character or paragraph formatting.

Reset Quick Styles

If you decide that you don't want to use the quick style set you applied to the document, you can remove it and reset to its default settings.

1. Click the Home tab on the Ribbon and click the Change Styles button in the Styles group. Point to Style Set. There are two ways you can reset the quick style set:

   Reset to Quick Styles from Template: Resets quick styles to the styles included in the template attached to the document.

   Reset Document Quick Styles: Resets quick styles to any styles you have modified or added to the current document.

2. Select the reset option you want to use. The quick styles will reset accordingly.

Go ahead and practice applying a style!

You will need to access practice files in your course online for this lesson. We've placed instructions in the appendix of this book on page 213.

Creating a Style

A **style** is a group of format settings stored under a single name. Styles save a lot of time and ensure that your documents are formatted in a consistent manner.

There are five different types of styles:

Character: Includes any type of character formatting, such as font size or type, colors, and font effects.

Paragraph: Includes any type of paragraph formatting, such as paragraph, tab, border, and bullets and numbering formats.

Linked: A combination of character and paragraph formatting properties.

Table: Provides a consistent style for all borders, shading, alignment and fonts in tables.

List: Applies similar alignment, numbering or bullet characters and fonts to lists.

Creating a style

With Word's quick styles, you probably won't need to create new styles very often. But if the need arises, creating a style is quick and easy.

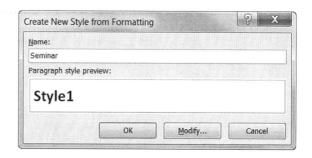

1. Select the text that contains the formatting of the new style.

2. Right-click the selection, select Styles, and select Save Selection as a New Quick Style from the contextual menu. The Create New Style from Formatting dialog box appears. You may add formatting or change formatting properties for the style here.

3. Click the Name text box and enter the style's name.

4. Click OK. The style will be added to the Quick Style Gallery.

Another way to create a style is to click the Home tab and click the Dialog Box Launcher in the Styles group. Click the New Style button in the Styles task pane and apply style formatting in the Create New Style from Formatting dialog box. Give the style a name and click OK.

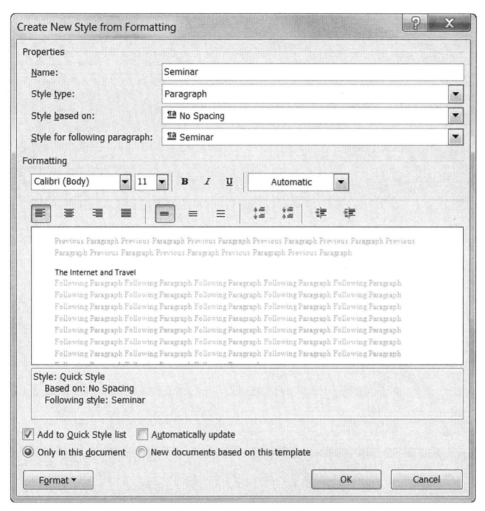

Using the files below, try creating a style yourself!

You will need to access practice files in your course online for this lesson. We've placed instructions in the appendix of this book on page 214.

I. **MATCHING.**
   Match the correct term to the definition.

1. *E* includes font size or type, colors, and font effects

2. *B* provides a style for borders and shading

3. *A* formats character and paragraph combination

4. *C* applies alignment and bullet characters to lists

5. *D* includes any paragraph formatting

A. linked
B. table
C. lists
D. paragraph
E. character

Modifying and Deleting a Style

If a style doesn't quite have the formatting attributes you would like, or if you created a style that you no longer want to use, styles are easily modified and deleted.

Modify a style

In most cases you won't need to change a style in a Quick Style set because the styles are designed to work together. Rather than modifying one of these built-in styles, you may want to consider creating a new style. Still, you may run into a situation where you want to modify a built-in style or a style that you've created.

1. Select text that uses the style you want to modify.

2. Apply the formatting you want to add to or remove from the style.

3. Right-click the style in the Styles Gallery and select Update [style name] to Match Selection from the contextual menu. The style will be modified to acquire the formatting properties of the selected text.

   Another way to modify a style is to right-click the style in the Styles Gallery and select Modify from the contextual menu. Or, click the Dialog Box Launcher in the Styles group, click the list arrow for the style you want to modify and select Modify. Edit the formatting of the style in the Modify Style dialog box.

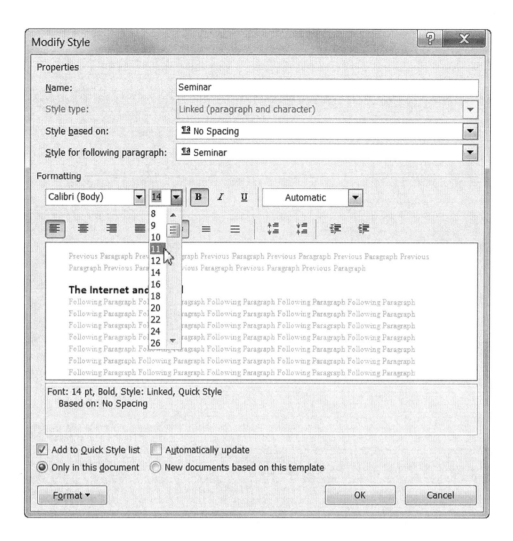

Delete a style

If a style is no longer needed, it may be deleted altogether.

1. Click the Dialog Box Launcher in the Styles group. The Styles task pane will appear.

2. Click the list arrow of the style you want to delete and select Delete [style name] or Revert to [style name] from the list. A dialog box will appear, asking to confirm deletion of the style.

3. Click Yes. The style will be deleted and the default "Normal" style, or a style similar to the deleted style, will be applied.

Tip: If there is no option to delete the style, Word may instruct you to revert to a similar style, which effectively deletes the style.

Try modifying or deleting a style with the help of the practice files below.

You will need to access practice files in your course online for this lesson. We've placed instructions in the appendix of this book on page 215.

Working with the Styles Gallery

The Styles Gallery makes it easy to view and access styles in a document. This lesson shows you how to organize which styles are displayed in the Styles Gallery.

Add a style to the Styles Gallery

If a style you want to use doesn't appear in the Styles Gallery, you can move it into the Styles Gallery so it is easily accessible.

1. Click the Home tab on the Ribbon and click the Dialog Box Launcher in the Styles group. The Styles task pane will appear.

2. Click the Options link. The Styles Gallery Options dialog box will appear.

3. Click the Select styles to show list arrow and select All styles. Click OK. The Styles task pane will display all the styles available in the document.

4. Point at the style you want to add to the Styles Gallery. Click the list arrow and select Add to Quick Style Gallery. The style will appear at the beginning of the Styles Gallery.

Remove a style from the Styles Gallery

Removing a style from the Styles Gallery does not remove the style from the document.

1. Click the Home tab on the Ribbon and right-click the style that you want to remove from the Styles Gallery in the Styles group. This will remove the style from the gallery, but it will still be available in the document.

2. Select Remove from Quick Style Gallery from the contextual menu. The style will no longer appear in the Styles Gallery.

Take a minute to practice working with the Styles Gallery.

You will need to access practice files in your course online for this lesson. We've placed instructions in the appendix of this book on page 216.

I. **TRUE/FALSE.**
   Mark the following true or false.

   1. Removing a style from the Styles Gallery removes the style from the document.
      ○ true
      ◉ false

   2. If a style you want to use doesn't appear in the Styles Gallery, you can move it into the Styles Gallery so it is easily accessible.
      ◉ true
      ○ false

   3. A fast way to remove a style is just to delete the text in the document that contains that style.
      ○ true
      ◉ false

Creating a New Quick Style Set

If you create a group of styles that you would like to use together, you can save them as a new quick style set.

1. Click the Home tab on the Ribbon and add and remove styles in the Styles Gallery. To create a quick style set, you can use a combination of styles you have created, and styles from other quick style sets. The styles that appear in the Styles Gallery will be included in the new quick style set.

2. Click the Change Styles button in the Styles group.

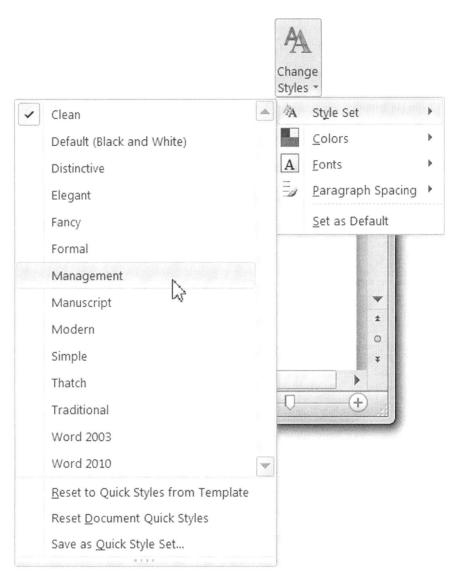

3. Point to Style Set and select Save as Quick Style Set. The Save Quick Style Set dialog box will appear.

4. Click in the File name text box and enter a name for the Quick Style Set. If you create other customized elements, use the same naming scheme so you can easily identify which parts are designed to go together.

5. Click Save. The quick style set will now appear in the Change Styles button list with the other built-in quick style sets.

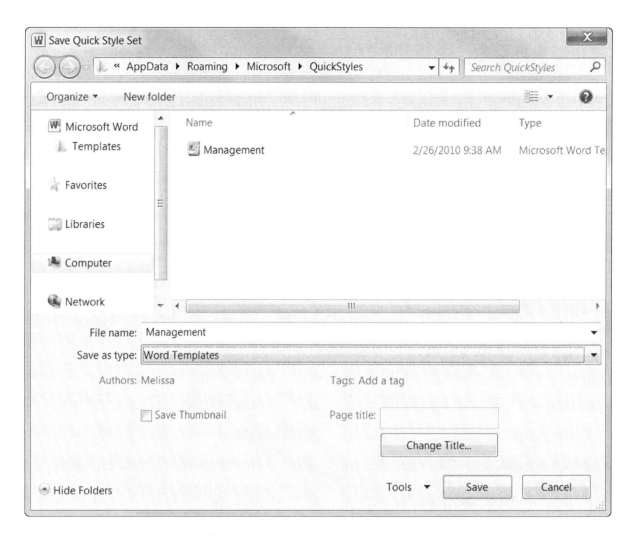

Create a new quick style set using the files below.

You will need to access practice files in your course online for this lesson. We've placed instructions in the appendix of this book on page 217.

Selecting, Removing, and Printing Styles

Styles form a bond between text that uses the same style. Use this common bond to work with text.

Select text that uses the same style

You can select all occurrences of a style in a document.

1. Click the Home tab on the Ribbon and right-click the style in the Styles Gallery in the Styles group.

2. Select All Instance(s). When the text is selected, you can work with the text as usual, such as to apply a different style, modify the style, or add formatting.

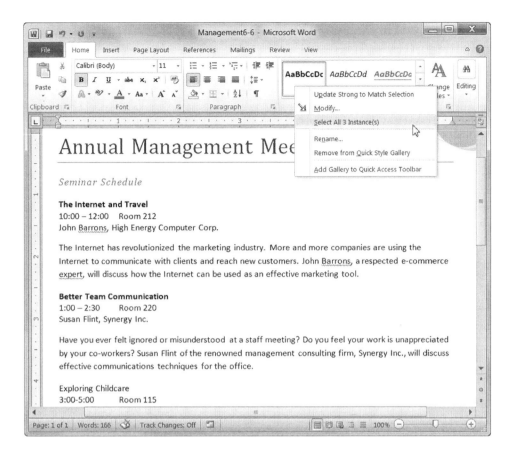

Remove a style from text

If you change your mind about using a style, you can easily remove the style from all text in the document.

1. Click the Home tab on the Ribbon and click the Dialog Box Launcher in the Styles group. The Styles task pane will appear.

2. Click the list arrow for the style you want to remove and select Clear Formatting of All Instance(s). The style will be removed from text in the document.

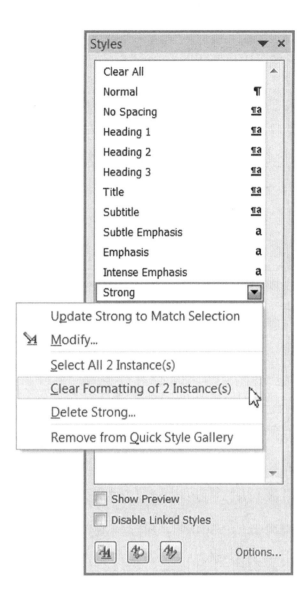

Print styles

You can print a summary of all the styles in a document, which includes a description of each style's properties and settings.

1. Click the File tab and select Print. The Print tab appears.

2. Click the Print all pages list arrow and select Styles.

3. Click Print.

Highlights

You must turn on the Keep track of formatting option to select, remove, or print styles. To do this, click the File tab and select Options. Click the Advanced tab and make sure the Keep track of formatting check box is selected.

Take the opportunity to try working with print styles using the instructions below.

You will need to access practice files in your course online for this lesson. We've placed instructions in the appendix of this book on page 218.

Comparing and Cleaning Up Styles

The Style Inspector helps identify styles and other formatting in the document.

Clean up styles

If text isn't updating to style changes the way you expected, or if text is not included in a style selection as you anticipated, it may not be formatted with a style.

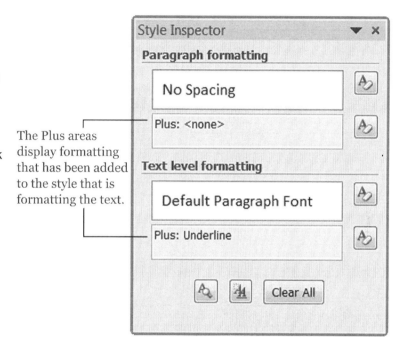

The Plus areas display formatting that has been added to the style that is formatting the text.

1. Click the Home tab on the Ribbon and click the Dialog Box Launcher in the Styles group. The Styles task pane will appear.

2. Click the Style Inspector button in the Styles task pane. The Style Inspector will appear.

3. Click the text you want to check or clean up. The Style Inspector will show the underlying paragraph and character styles that are used in the current text. If the Plus: area below the paragraph or character style references other formatting properties, those formatting properties have been added manually and are not part of the underlying style.

4. Use the controls in the Style Inspector to clear all styles and formatting, create a new style, or reveal formatting.

Compare formatted text to other formatted text

Comparing text makes it easier for you to identify the formatting attributes applied to text.

1. Click the Home tab on the Ribbon and click the Dialog Box Launcher in the Styles group. The Styles task pane will appear.

2. Click the Style Inspector button in the Styles task pane. The Style Inspector will appear.

3. Click the Reveal Formatting button. The Reveal Formatting task pane will appear.

4. Click or select text to view its formatting. The formatting properties of the selected text will be displayed in the Reveal Formatting task pane.

5. Click the Compare to another selection check box in the Reveal Formatting task pane. Now you can compare the formatting of the selected text to other text in the document. Notice that when the text is compared to itself, there are no formatting differences.

6. Click or select the text to compare to the previously selected text. The formatting differences between the two instances will be displayed in the Reveal Formatting task pane.

7. Close the Reveal Formatting task pane and Style Inspector when you are finished.

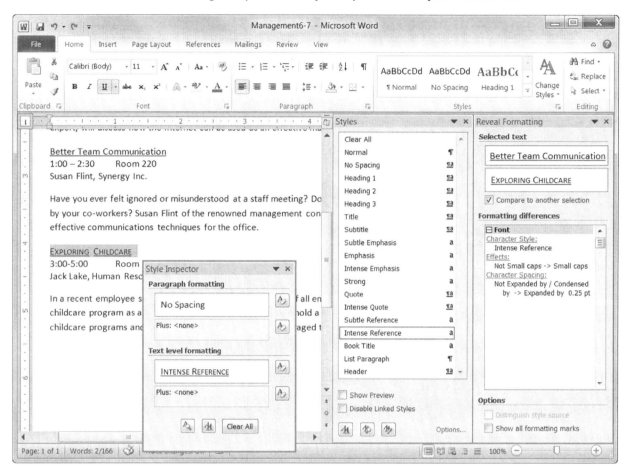

The files below will help you practice comparing and cleaning up styles.

You will need to access practice files in your course online for this lesson. We've placed instructions in the appendix of this book on page 219.

I. **TRUE/FALSE.**

Mark the following true or false.

1. The Plus area displays formatting that has been added to the style that is formatting the text.
   - ⊙ true
   - ○ false

2. Comparing text makes it easy to identify the formatting attributes which have been applied to the text.
   - ⊙ true
   - ○ false

3. The Style Inspector doesn't help with comparing text or formatting text attributes.
   - ○ true
   - ⊙ false

Applying Document Themes

Word 2010's document themes provide a consistent and professional look for your documents. Each document theme consists of three design elements:

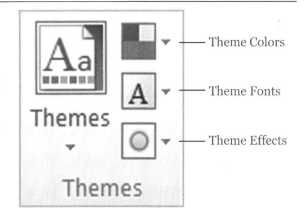

Theme Colors: A set of eight coordinated colors used in formatting text and objects in the document.

Theme Fonts: A set of coordinated heading and body font types.

Theme Effects: A set of coordinated formatting properties for shapes and objects.

Tips: Document themes work best when saved in .docx files. They may not display correctly in .doc format.

Apply a document theme

Applying a document theme affects all elements of the document: colors, fonts, and effects.

1. Click the Page Layout tab on the Ribbon and click the Themes button in the Themes group. A list of built-in document themes will appear. The default theme is "Office," which is highlighted in orange.

2. Select the document theme you want to apply. The formatting associated with the document theme will be applied to the document.

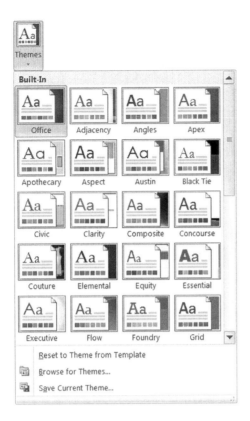

Tip: If the theme you want to use doesn't appear in the list, you may browse for additional themes on Office Online by clicking Search Office Online. Or, if a theme is saved elsewhere on your computer or network location, click Browse for Themes to go to the theme's location.

Mix and match document themes

You are not bound to the colors, fonts, or effects that are assigned to a document theme. You may customize document themes by mixing and matching theme colors, theme fonts, and theme effects.

1. Click the Page Layout tab on the Ribbon.

2. Click the Theme Colors, Theme Fonts, or Theme Effects button in the Themes group and select the colors, fonts, or effects you want to use. The change will be applied to the document. The document theme won't change, but it will no longer be applied.

Practice applying a document theme! It's easy!

> You will need to access practice files in your course online for this lesson. We've placed instructions in the appendix of this book on page 220.

I. **FILL IN THE BLANK.**
   Enter the correct word in the blank provided.

1. The built-in list of _document themes_ in Word coordinates colors, fonts, and shape effects.

2. _Theme fonts_ are sets of coordinated heading and body font types.

3. You may _Customize_ document themes by mixing and matching until you find the ones you want together.

4. A set of coordinated formatting properties for shapes and objects describes the _theme effects_

Creating New Theme Colors and Fonts

You will probably be able to find a document theme that suits your needs among Word's built-in options. While you can't create your own theme effects, you can create your own customized theme colors and fonts.

1. Click the Page Layout tab on the Ribbon and click the Theme Colors or Theme Fonts button in the Themes group.

2. Select Create New Theme Colors or Create New Theme Fonts from the list. A dialog box will appear where you can select the colors and fonts you want to use.

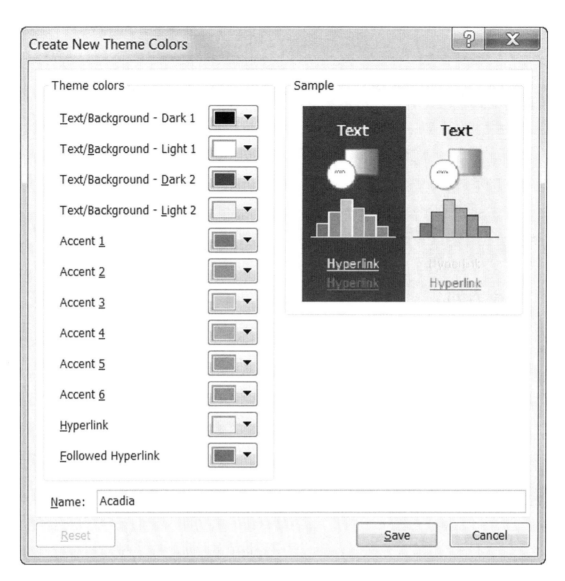

3. Select the colors and fonts you want to use.

4. Click the Name text box and type a name for the new color or font theme. If you want to coordinate new theme colors and fonts, save them under the same name, just as they are with built-in themes.

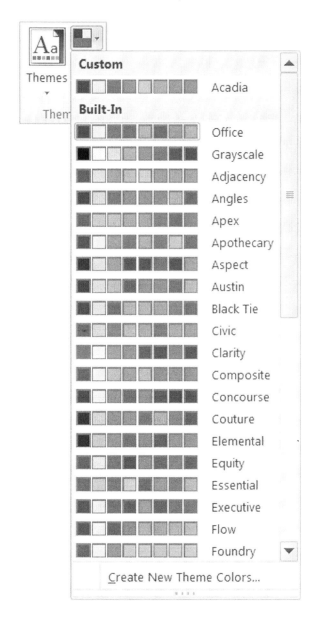

Theme elements that you have created appear in a special Custom section at the top of the list.

5. Click Save. If you want to use the new colors and fonts together, save them under the same name so that it is easy to identify that they go together.

Tip: To edit a custom theme color or font, click the Theme Color or Theme Font button. Right-click the theme color or font and select Edit. To remove a custom theme color or font, click the Theme Color or Theme Font button. Right-click the option you want to delete and select Delete. Click Yes to confirm the deletion.

Highlights

The colors and fonts that appear in the dialog box are based on the previously selected theme. Click the element you want to change and select More Colors for additional color options.

Using the files below, practice creating new theme colors.

You will need to access practice files in your course online for this lesson. We've placed instructions in the appendix of this book on page 221.

Save a New Document Theme

You can use theme fonts or colors that you have created to create an entire document theme. For example, you could create a document theme that uses specific colors and fonts for your organization.

You can save any combination of theme colors, theme fonts, and theme effects as a new document theme. When you save a new document theme, it becomes available in all Office programs.

1. Apply the theme colors, fonts, and effects you want to use in the new document theme to the document. This can be a combination of items you have created, and built-in items.

2. Click the Page Layout tab on the Ribbon and click the Themes button in the Themes group. A list of built-in themes appears.

3. Select Save Current Theme. The Save Current Theme dialog box appears. When you give the new document theme a name, use a naming scheme similar to other items, such as the theme colors or fonts, so that it is easy to identify that they go together.

4. Click the File name text box, enter a name, and click the Save button. The document theme is now available under the Themes button in the Themes group.

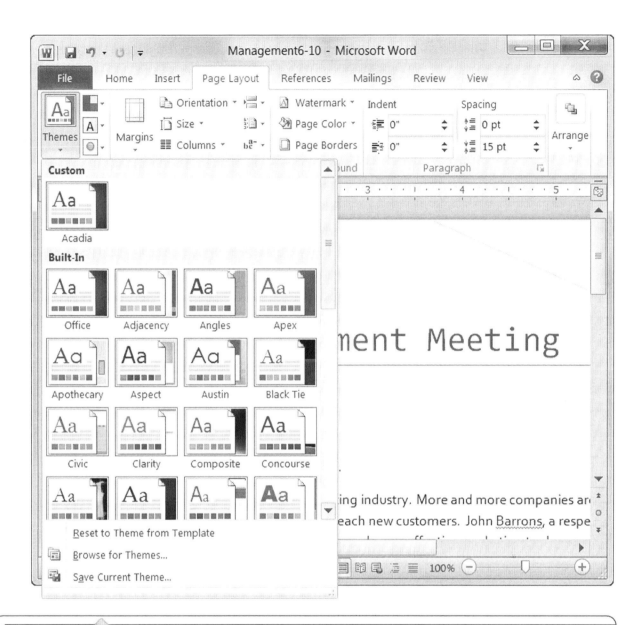

Highlights

To remove a custom document theme, click the Themes button. Right-click the custom theme and select Delete. Click Yes to confirm the deletion.

Go ahead and practice saving a document theme. All the instructions you need are below.

You will need to access practice files in your course online for this lesson. We've placed instructions in the appendix of this book on page 222.

Unit 8
Working with Tables

Working with Tables – Introduction

Tables rank right up there with the spell checker as one of the neatest word processing features. A table neatly arranges text and data in a grid, organized by columns and rows. Once you have entered information in a table, you can do all kinds of things with it. For example, you can sort the information alphabetically or numerically; add and delete columns and/or rows; and make your table stand out by formatting it with border, shading, and color options. Tables can be used in place of tab stops to organize and layout information in an attractive, organized manner.

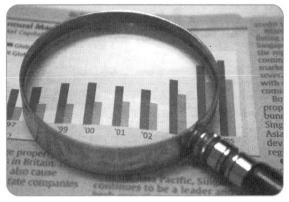

As powerful as tables are, most people don't know how to use them effectively, if at all. Tables are so important that this entire unit is devoted to helping you become a table expert.

Creating a Table

Tables are very useful tools in creating and formatting documents. For example, with a table you can:

Align Text, Numbers, and Graphics: Tables make it easy to align text, numbers, and graphics in columns and rows. Many users prefer using tables to align text instead of tab stops, because text can wrap to multiple lines in a table.

Create a Form: You can use tables to store lists of telephone numbers, clients, and employee rosters.

Share Information: You can use tables to share information between programs. For example, you can copy and paste a table's information into a Microsoft Excel worksheet or Access database.

Create a Publication: Tables make it easier to create calendars, brochures, business cards, and many other publications.

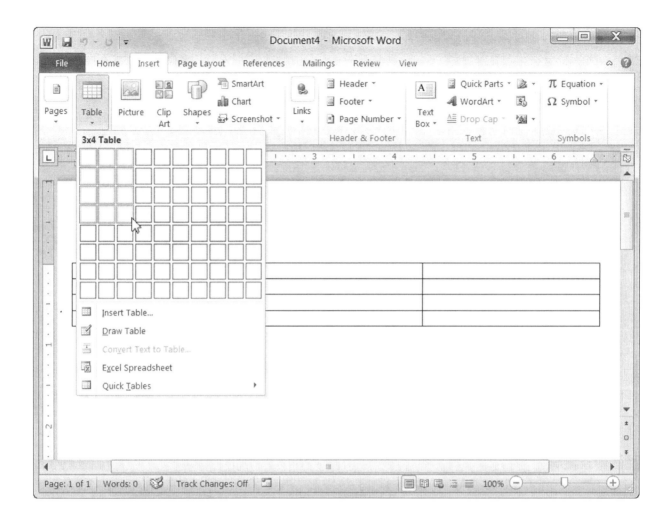

Insert a table

To create a table, you must first specify how many columns (which run up and down) and rows (which run left to right) you want to appear in your table. Cells are small, rectangular shaped boxes where the rows and columns intersect. The number of columns and rows determines the number of cells in a table. If you don't know exactly how many columns and rows you want in your table, take an educated guess—you can always add or delete columns and rows later.

1. Click the Insert tab on the Ribbon and click the Table button in the Tables group. A grid will appear, representing rows and columns in the table. As you move the cursor inside the grid, the number of rows and columns that will appear in the table is updated at the top of the list. A preview of how the table will look in the document also appears as you drag your cursor across the grid.

2. Select the number of columns and rows you want to create using the new table grid. The table will be inserted with the number of columns and rows you selected.

Another way to insert a table is to click the Insert tab on the Ribbon and click the Table button in the Tables group. Select Insert Table from the list and select the number of columns and rows you want to use in the Insert Table dialog box. Click OK.

The instructions below will help you create a table of your own.

> You will need to access practice files in your course online for this lesson. We've placed instructions in the appendix of this book on page 223.

Working with a Table

In order to work with a table, you need to learn a few basic skills: how to move the insertion point between cells, how to enter or edit table data, and how to select items.

Using the table you just created, try these exercises:

Move between cells

There are several ways to move between cells in a table:

- Click in a cell with the mouse.
- Use the up, down, left, and right arrow keys.
- Press TAB to move forward one field or cell, and press SHIFT + TAB to move back one field or cell.

Enter or edit information in a table

1. Click a cell in the table. The insertion point will appear in the cell.
2. Enter or edit text or numerical data, as desired. If you enter more text than fits in a cell, the cell height will expand automatically to hold it.

Select cells, rows, columns, and tables

Just like other elements in Word, you have to select the parts of a table in order to work with them.

1. Position the insertion point in the cell, row, or column you want to select.
2. Under Table Tools on the Ribbon, click the Layout tab and click the Select button in the Table group.
3. Choose the table item you want to select: Cell, Column, Row, or Table. You can also do the following to select:

   Cells: Click the left edge of the cell.

   Multiple Cells: Drag across the cell, row, or column. Or select a single cell, row, or column and hold down the SHIFT key while you click another cell, row, or column.

   Row: Click to the left of the row (outside of the table).

   Column: Click the column's top border (the pointer will change).

   Table: Click the move handle next to the table (must be in Print Layout view).

Try working with a table using the file and instructions below.

You will need to access practice files in your course online for this lesson. We've placed instructions in the appendix of this book on page 224.

I. FILL IN THE BLANK.
Enter the correct word in the blank provided.

1. Dragging across a cell, row, or column will select _____.

2. To move back one cell in a table, press _____.

3. To select a row, click to the _____ of it, outside of the table.

Resizing and Moving a Table

You can quickly and easily resize or move a table in Word.

Resize a table

You can use the mouse to resize a table.

1. Make sure you are in Print Layout view.

2. Click anywhere inside the table, if necessary. The table's resize handle will appear in the lower right-hand corner of the table until the table is the desired size. As you resize the table, a dotted outline appears to show you the new outline of the table.

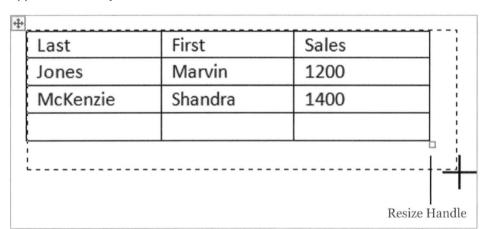

Last	First	Sales
Jones	Marvin	1200
McKenzie	Shandra	1400

Resize Handle

Move a table

Moving a table is very similar to resizing it.

1. Make sure you are in Print Layout view.

2. Click anywhere inside the table, if necessary. The table's move handle will appear in the upper left-hand corner of the table.

3. Click and drag the table's move handle to a new location on the page. As you move the table, a dotted outline will appear to show you the new location of the table.

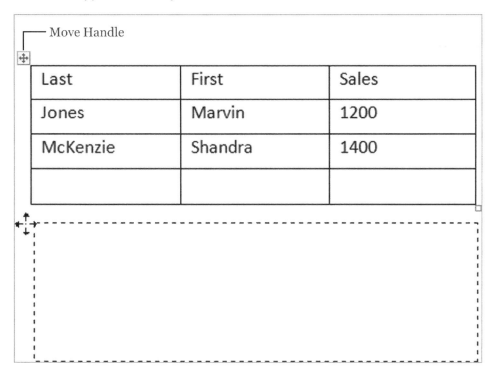

Now, try resizing and moving tables on your own!

> You will need to access practice files in your course online for this lesson. We've placed instructions in the appendix of this book on page 225.

Adjusting Table Alignment and Text Wrapping

In the Table Properties dialog box, you can adjust the alignment of a table within the document, as well as the way document text wraps around a table.

If your table is as wide as the page, or if you don't have any text in the surrounding document, you won't notice any difference between the alignment or text wrapping options, respectively.

Highlights

The Table Properties dialog box also includes tabs for Row, Column, and Cell properties. Here you can adjust row and column size, as well as individual cell size and alignment of cell contents.

1. Select the table.

2. Under Table Tools on the Ribbon, click the Layout tab and click the Properties button in the Table group. The Table Properties dialog box will appear.

3. Select the Table tab if it isn't already selected. Here you can adjust table alignment within the document—select from Left, Center, or Right alignment—as well as whether or not you want the document text to wrap around the table.

4. Select an Alignment or Text wrapping option and click OK. The table alignment or text wrapping will be adjusted.

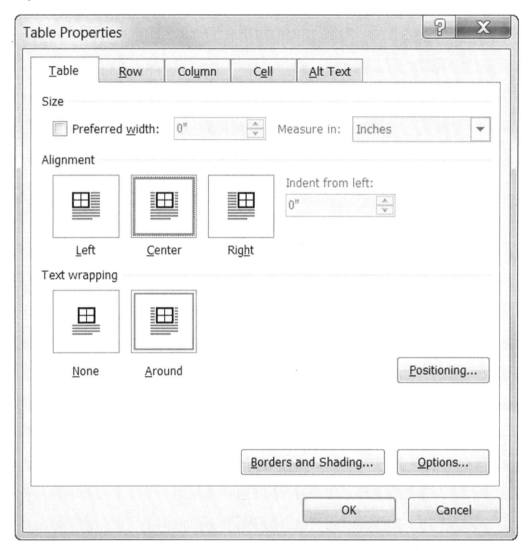

Tip: Click the Options, Positioning, or Borders and Shading buttons for even more detailed table options.

Practice adjusting table alignment and text wrapping on the table attached below.

You will need to access practice files in your course online for this lesson. We've placed instructions in the appendix of this book on page 226.

Working with Cell Formatting

In this lesson, you will learn how to align text horizontally and vertically in a cell, change text direction, and adjust cell margins.

Align cell contents

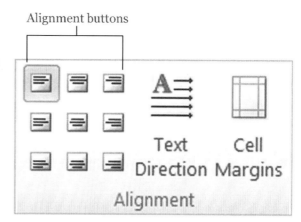

1. Select the cell(s) containing information you want to align. The Design and Layout tabs will appear under the Table Tools on the Ribbon.

2. Under Table Tools on the Ribbon, click the Layout tab and click an alignment button in the Alignment group.

    You can also align cells by selecting the cell(s), right-clicking, and selecting Cell Alignment from the contextual menu and selecting an alignment.

Change text direction

1. Select the cell(s). The Design and Layout tabs will appear under the Table Tools on the Ribbon.

2. Under Table Tools on the Ribbon, click the Layout tab and click the Text Direction button in the Alignment group. The text direction for the selected cell(s) will change.

3. Click the Text Direction button again to cycle through available directions. You can also change text direction by selecting the cell(s), right-clicking, and selecting Text Direction from the contextual menu. Select an orientation from the Text Direction dialog box.

Last	First	Sales	
Jones	Marvin	1200	
McKenzie	Shandra	1400	

Adjust cell margins

You can adjust how much space appears between a cell's contents and its borders by adjusting cell margins.

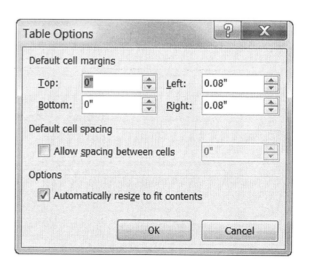

1. Click anywhere inside the table. The Design and Layout tabs will appear under the Table Tools on the Ribbon.

2. Under Table Tools on the Ribbon, click the Layout tab and click the Cell Margins button in the Alignment group. The Table Options dialog box will appear.

3. Adjust the cell margins and click OK. Not only can you change the distance from the cell contents to

the cell borders, but you can also separate individual cells from other cells in the table by adjusting the Default cell spacing area of the dialog box.

Tip: Adjusting cell margins changes the margins of the current table and all subsequent tables. Your changes become the default settings for all tables.

Formatting cells is pretty easy! Give it a try using the files below.

You will need to access practice files in your course online for this lesson. We've placed instructions in the appendix of this book on pages 227-228.

I. TRUE/FALSE.
Mark the following true or false.

1. You can adjust how much space is between a cell's contents and its borders by adjusting text direction.

   ○ true
   ◉ false

2. One way to align a cell is to select the cell, right-click, and select Cell Alignment.

   ◉ true
   ○ false

3. Clicking the Layout tab and then Cell Margins will change cell contents.

   ○ true
   ◉ false

Merging and Splitting Cells and Tables

You can adjust the number of cells that appear in a table by merging and splitting cells. You can also split a table into two tables. Knowing how to merge and split cells is absolutely necessary when creating complex tables.

Merge cells

The merge cells command combines several smaller cells into a single larger cell that spans the space that the previous cells occupied.

1. Select the cells you want to merge.

2. Under Table Tools on the Ribbon, click the Layout tab and click the Merge Cells button in the Merge group. You can also select the cells you want to merge, then right-click and select Merge Cells from the contextual menu.

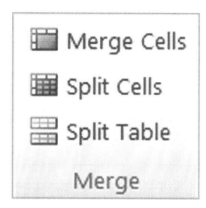

Split a cell

Cells can also be broken up into several smaller cells by using the Split Cells command.

1. Select the cell you want to split.

2. Under Table Tools on the Ribbon, click the Layout tab and click the Split Cells button in the Merge group. You can also select the cell you want to split, then right-click and select Split Cells from the contextual menu.

3. Specify how you want to split the cell in the Split Cells dialog box and click OK.

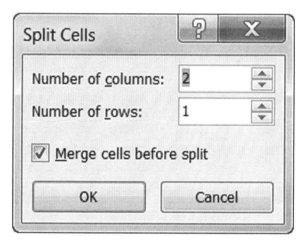

Split a table

You can also split a table into two separate tables.

1. Select the table row where you want to split the table. The row you select will become the first row of the new table.

2. Under Table Tools on the Ribbon, click the Layout tab and click the Split Table button in the Merge group. The table will be split into two tables. If the new table overlaps or obstructs the original table, you may need to move the tables in order to view them.

Before		
Last	First	Sales
Jones	Marvin	1200
McKenzie	Shandra	1400

After		
Last	First	Sales
Jones	Marvin	1200
McKenzie	Shandra	1400

Try your hand at merging and splitting cells!

You will need to access practice files in your course online for this lesson. We've placed instructions in the appendix of this book on page 229.

Inserting and Deleting Rows and Columns

In this lesson, you will learn how to delete entire columns and rows and how to insert new columns and rows. You'll also learn how you can repeat the header row on tables that span multiple pages.

Insert a row

1. Place your insertion point in the row that is above or below where you want to insert the new row.

2. Under Table Tools on the Ribbon, click the Layout tab and click the Insert Above or Insert Below button in the Rows & Columns group.

   Another way to insert a row is to place the insertion point in the bottom-right cell of the table and press TAB to insert a new row at the bottom of the table. You can also right-click a row, point to Insert, and select Insert Rows Above or Insert Rows Below from the contextual menu.

Insert a column

1. Place your insertion point in the table in the column that is left or right of where you want to insert the new column.

2. Under Table Tools on the Ribbon, click the Layout tab and click the Insert Left button or the Insert Right button in the Rows & Columns group.

Another way to insert a column is to right-click and point to Insert and select Insert Columns to the Left or Insert Columns to the Right from the contextual menu.

Delete a row or column

1. Select the column(s) or row(s) you want to delete.

2. Under Table Tools on the Ribbon, click the Layout tab and click the Delete button in the Rows & Columns group.

3. Select Delete Rows or Delete Columns from the list.

   You can also delete rows or columns by selecting the row(s) or column(s), right-clicking, and selecting Delete Rows or Delete Columns.

Tip: You can also delete individual cells in a table. Select the cell(s) you want to delete and click the Delete button in the Rows & Columns group. Select Delete Cells and click OK.

Repeat header rows

If you have a table that extends across several pages, you can repeat the header row at the top of each page of the table.

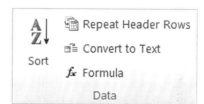

1. Select the rows you want to use as headings.

2. Click the Layout tab under Table Tools on the Ribbon.

3. Click the Repeat Header Rows button in the Data group.

   You can also keep a table row from breaking and separating the row's contents onto two pages. Right-click the table and select Table Properties from the contextual menu. On the Row tab of the Table Properties dialog box, deselect the Allow row to break across pages option.

Practice your new skills using the files below.

You will need to access practice files in your course online for this lesson. We've placed instructions in the appendix of this book on page 230.

I. **TRUE/FALSE.**
   Mark the following true or false.

1. One way to insert a column is to right-click and point to Insert and select Insert Columns to the Left.
   - ⦿ true
   - ◯ false

2. It is not possible to repeat the header row at the top of each page of a table.
   - ◯ true
   - ⦿ false

3. A shortcut for inserting a row in a table is pressing CTRL + R.
   - ◯ true
   - ⦿ false

Adjusting Row Height and Column Width

When you create a table, all of the rows and columns are the same size. As you enter information in a table, you will quickly discover that some of the rows and columns are not large enough to properly display the information they contain.

Table Column Width

AutoFit — 2.22" — Distribute Rows

0.18" — Distribute Columns

Cell Size

Table Column Height

Adjust row height

You will seldom need to change a row's height because, unless you specify otherwise, rows automatically expand to the tallest cell in the row—the one that contains the most lines of text.

1. Select the row(s).

2. Under Table Tools on the Ribbon, click the Layout tab.

3. Specify the row height in the Height text box in the Cell Size group. You can also adjust row height by clicking and dragging the row's bottom border up or down (in the Print Layout view).

Tip: You can distribute selected rows evenly so they are the same height. Select the rows, click the Layout tab under Table Tools and click the Distribute Rows button in the Cell Size group.

Adjust column width

1. Select the column(s).

2. Under Table Tools on the Ribbon, click the Layout tab.

3. Click the Table Column Width text box in the Cell Size group and specify the column width.

Another way to adjust column width is (while in the Print Layout view) to click and drag the column's right border to the left or right. You can also either double-click the column's right border or click the AutoFit button and select an option to automatically resize the columns to fit their contents or the size of the window.

Tip: You can distribute columns evenly so that they are the same width. Select the columns, click the Layout tab under Table Tools and click the Distribute Columns button in the Cell Size group.

Adjusting rows and columns will help you make great looking tables. Practice using the files below.

You will need to access practice files in your course online for this lesson. We've placed instructions in the appendix of this book on page 231

Using Table Drawing Tools

In Word, you can draw and modify tables the same way you would use a pencil to draw a table on a piece of paper. You may find the table drawing tools to be especially helpful when creating or modifying complicated or irregular tables.

Draw borders

1. Under Table Tools on the Ribbon, click the Design tab and click the Draw Table button in the Draw Borders group. The pointer will change to look like a pencil.
2. Click and drag to draw boundaries, rows, columns, or table cells. Use the Line Style, Line Weight, and Pen Color commands in the Draw Borders group to determine how the borders appear.

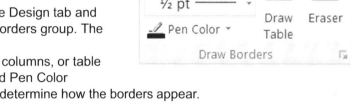

Erase borders

1. Under Table Tools on the Ribbon, click the Design tab and click the Eraser button in the Draw Borders group. The pointer will change to look like an eraser.
2. Click and drag across table lines to erase the lines. The border is erased.

Last	First	Sales
Jones	Marvin	1200
McKenzie	Shandra	1400

Using the files below, try out the table drawing tools.

You will need to access practice files in your course online for this lesson. We've placed instructions in the appendix of this book on page 232.

Working with Sorting and Formulas

Word provides many options for working with table data. You can sort table data into a more useful order, and even perform calculations by inserting formulas into table cells.

Sort table data

Word can sort data in a list alphabetically, numerically, or chronologically (by date). In addition, Word can sort information in ascending (A to Z) or descending (Z to A) order. You can sort an entire table or a portion of a table by selecting what you want to sort.

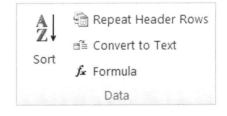

1. Select the cells or information you want to sort. Usually, you'll want to select the header row along with the rows you want to sort.

2. Under Table Tools on the Ribbon, click the Layout tab, and click the Sort button in the Data group. The Sort dialog box will appear.

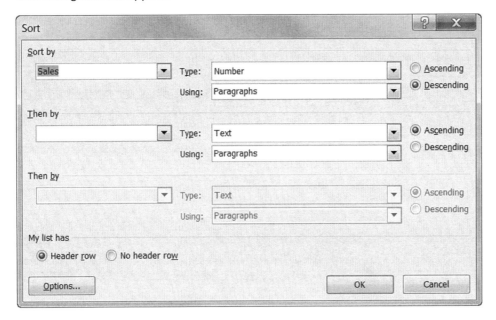

3. Define how you want to sort the data and click OK.

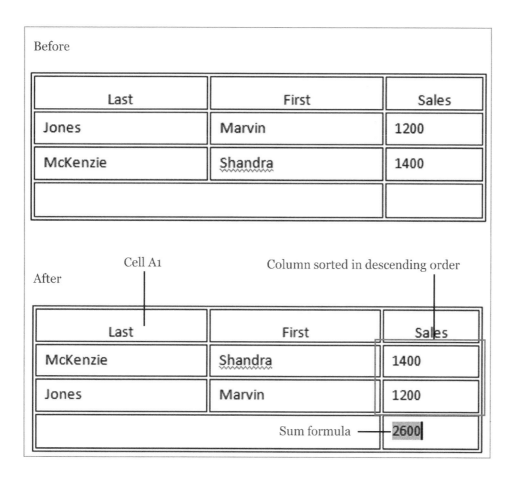

Before

Last	First	Sales
Jones	Marvin	1200
McKenzie	Shandra	1400

Cell A1   Column sorted in descending order

After

Last	First	Sales
McKenzie	Shandra	1400
Jones	Marvin	1200
	Sum formula	2600

Use formulas in a table

Word is not a spreadsheet program like Microsoft Excel, which is made to perform calculations, but it can do some simple arithmetic. To enter your own calculations, called formulas in Word, you can use the Formula dialog box, and you can refer to the cells in a table using cell references. A cell reference identifies where a cell is located in a table.

Although tables don't have visible headers identifying the rows and columns, every cell reference uses a letter (A, B, C and so on) to represent its column and a number (1, 2, 3 and so on) to represent its row. A1, B3, and D5 are all examples of cell references.

Instead of entering specific cell references you want to sum, you can use a reference such as ABOVE, which indicates all the cells above the cell containing the formula.

1. Place the insertion point in a blank table cell where you want to insert the formula.

2. Under Table Tools on the Ribbon, click the Layout tab and click the Formula button in the Data group. The Formula dialog box will appear appears.

3. Enter the formula in the Formula box. For example, =SUM(C2, C3) calculates the sum of table cells C2 and C3. Use the Number format list arrow to define how the formula result appears. Use the Paste function list arrow to build a formula using built-in functions.

4. Click OK. The formula result will appear in the cell.

Highlights

Remember: All formulas start with an equal sign (=), followed by a function name (such as SUM), followed by parentheses containing the location of the cells on which you want to perform the calculation.

Besides regular cell references, you can use terms that describe the location of cells in a table, such as Above or Left, which reference all cells above or to the left, respectively, of the selected cell. For example, =SUM(ABOVE) totals all the cells above the selected cell in a table.

If you change a value in a Word table, you'll need to recalculate the formulas manually.

Try working with a little table data on your own. The instructions below will guide you.

You will need to access practice files in your course online for this lesson. We've placed instructions in the appendix of this book on page 233.

I. MULTIPLE CHOICE.
Choose the best answer.

1. All formulas start with a(n) (●equal sign, ○function name).

2. Formulas (○do, ●do not) recalculate automatically in Word.

3. Word can sort information in (●ascending and descending, ○only ascending) order.

4. Every cell reference uses a (●letter, ○number) to represent its column and a [5.](○letter, ●number) to represent its row.

Working with Borders and Shading

Borders improve a table's appearance, giving it a polished, professional look. Borders can make it easier to read the information in a table, especially when the information is numerical. Adding shading to a table is similar to adding borders—you select the cells and then select shading options.

Apply a table border

When you create a table, Word automatically adds borders or lines around every cell in the table, but it's very easy to change, add, or remove your table's borders.

1. Select the cells where you want to adjust the borders. The Table Tools will appear on the Ribbon. To select the whole table, click the table's move handle.

2. Under Table Tools on the Ribbon, click the Design tab and click the Borders list arrow. Here you can choose from several border options. You can select No Border to remove a border from the selection.

3. Select the border type you want to apply to the selected cells. The border will be applied.

Another way to apply a table border is to select the cells where you want to apply a border. Under Table Tools on the Ribbon, click the Design tab and click the Borders list arrow. Select Borders and Shading from the list. You can also right-click the selection and select Borders and Shading from the contextual menu. Use the commands on the Borders tab in the Borders and Shading dialog box.

View gridlines

Gridlines are dashed lines that show you the location of the table cell borders. They do not appear by default. You can easily display and hide table gridlines, but the gridlines won't be visible if the table is in the default table format because the black border covers the gridlines.

Last	First	Sales
McKenzie	Shandra	1400
Jones	Marvin	1200
		2600

1. Select a table.

2. Under Table Tools on the Ribbon, click the Layout tab and click the View Gridlines button in the Table group. Gridlines will be displayed in all tables in the document. Note that gridlines do not print.

3. To hide the gridlines, click the View Gridlines button again. The gridlines will be hidden.

Apply a fill color

Shading includes fill colors and also patterns that you can apply to table cells.

Last	First	Sales
McKenzie	Shandra	1400
Jones	Marvin	1200
		2600

1. Select the cells where you want to apply a fill color. The Table Tools will appear on the Ribbon.

2. Under Table Tools on the Ribbon, click the Design tab and click the Shading list arrow in the Table Styles group. A palette of fill colors will appear.

3. Select a fill color from the list. The color will be applied.

Apply a pattern

1. Select the cells where you want to apply a pattern.

2. Under Table Tools on the Ribbon, click the Design tab and click the Borders button list arrow in the Table Styles group. Select Borders and Shading. The Borders and Shading dialog box will appear.

   You can also right-click the selection and select Borders and Shading from the contextual menu.

3. Click the Shading tab, click the Style list arrow in the Patterns area and select a pattern style. You can also adjust the colors of patterns here.

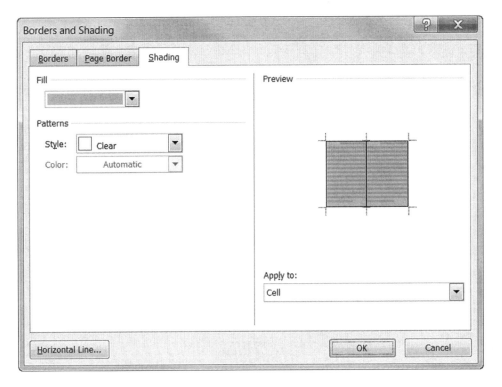

4. Click the Color list arrow and select a pattern color. Here you will see a preview of the pattern.

5. Click OK.

Add some borders and shading to a table using the instructions below.

> You will need to access practice files in your course online for this lesson. We've placed instructions in the appendix of this book on page 234.

I. MULTIPLE CHOICE.
Choose the best answer.

1. Which of the following is not true about gridlines?
   ○ They are dashed lines that show you the location of the table cell borders.
   ○ They do not print.
   ○ You can display and hide them.
   ● They are visible if the table is in the default table format.

2. To select a whole table, _____.
   ○ press CTRL + A
   ● click the table's move handle
   ○ press CTRL + T
   ○ double-click a cell

3. Fill in the next step when applying a fill color: "Under Table Tools on the Ribbon, click the Design tab and then click the _____ list arrow in the Table Styles group."

◉ Shading
○ Palette
○ Color
○ Apply

4. To remove a border after you have applied it, _____.

○ select Delete Border
○ press CTRL + D
◉ select No Border
○ highlight the table and press Backspace

Using Table Styles

You can easily spice up your tables by applying built-in table formatting styles. You can also use styles in the Styles group on the Home tab to apply styles to the text inside a table. These can be applied in addition to a table style.

Apply a table style

By default, a table is created with the Table Grid style, which includes a basic black border around each cell in the table. Word includes many built-in styles that include more interesting formatting.

Table styles   More button

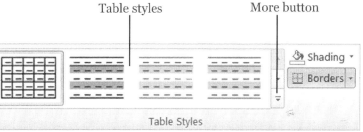

Table Styles

1. Select the table.

2. Under Table Tools on the Ribbon, click the Design tab. Here you can see the Table Styles group. You can use the arrow buttons to scroll through the table styles in the gallery.

3. Select the style you want to use in the Table Styles group. To display the entire Table Styles gallery, click the More button in the Table Styles group.

Remove a table style

You can easily remove table styles.

1. Select the table from which you want to remove the style. The Design tab will appear.

2. Under Table Tools on the Ribbon, click the Design tab and click the More button in the Table Styles group.

3. Select Clear. The Table Normal style, which doesn't have any formatting, will be applied.

Create a custom table style

You can also create a new, custom table style that meets your exact specifications.

1. Select the table you want to format with a style.

2. Under Table Tools on the Ribbon, click the Design tab and click the More button in the Table Styles group.

3. Select New Table Style. The Create New Style from Formatting dialog box will appear.

4. Select the formatting attributes you want to use in the new table style and click OK. The new style will appear in the Custom area of the Table Styles gallery in the Table Styles group.

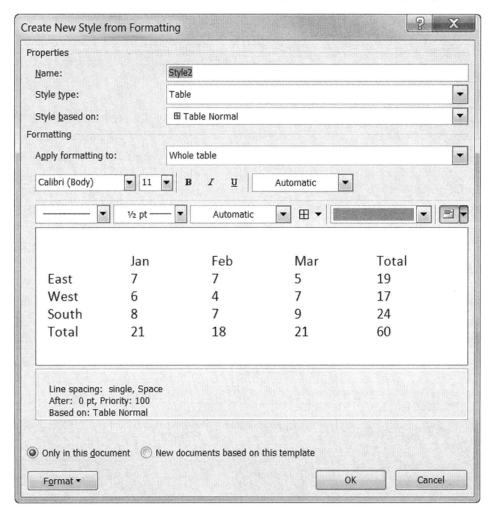

Tip: You can make the new table style available only in the current document or for new documents as well. Select either the Only in this document or the New documents based on this template option in the dialog box.

Highlights

You can also modify an existing table style. Apply the style you want to modify, then click the More button in the Table Styles group and select Modify Table Style. Modify the table properties and click OK.

Practice using some different table styles using the files below.

You will need to access practice files in your course online for this lesson. We've placed instructions in the appendix of this book on page 235.

Using Table Style Options

Besides applying table styles, you can format individual table style elements.

1. Select the table.
2. Under Table Tools on the Ribbon, click the Design tab. The formatting options available in the Table Style Options group include:

   Header Row: Displays special formatting for the first row of the table.

   Total Row: Displays special formatting for the last row of the table.

   First/Last Column: Displays special formatting for the first or last columns in the table.

   Banded Rows/Columns: Displays odd and even rows and columns differently for easier reading.

With banded rows

Last	First	Sales
McKenzie	Shandra	1400
Jones	Marvin	1200
		2600

Without banded rows

Last	First	Sales
McKenzie	Shandra	1400
Jones	Marvin	1200
		2600

☑ Header Row   ☑ First Column
☐ Total Row   ☐ Last Column
☑ Banded Rows ☐ Banded Columns
Table Style Options

3. Select the option(s) you want to use in the Table Style Options group.

Now that you know what your table style options are, give a few a try!

You will need to access practice files in your course online for this lesson. We've placed instructions in the appendix of this book on page 236.

I. MATCHING.
Match the correct table formatting option to the definition.

1. A   displays formatting for first and last columns in a table
2. C   displays formatting for the first row of a table
3. B   displays odd and even rows and columns differently
4. D   displays formatting for the last row of a table

A. First/Last Column
B. Banded Rows/Columns
C. Header Row
D. Total Row

Converting or Deleting a Table

If you don't want table data to appear in a table any longer, preferring that the contents are part of the other text of the document, you can convert a table to text. You can also simply delete a table.

Convert a table to text

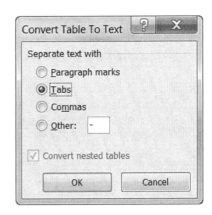

1. Place your insertion point in the table

2. Under Table Tools on the Ribbon, click the Layout tab and click the Convert to Text button in the Data group. The Convert Table To Text dialog box will appear.

3. Select the character you want to use to separate the text contained in each cell. You can select one of the options to separate text or define your own separation character in the dialog box.

4. Click OK. The table will disappear and the table's contents will appear as document text—although the text is contained inside a frame. The contents of each table cell are separated by the character you selected.

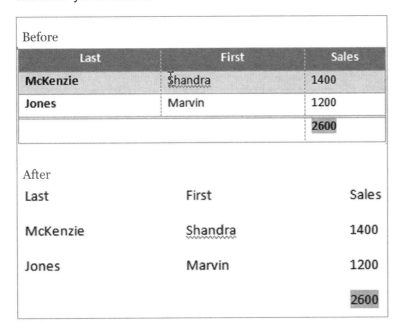

Delete a table

1. Place your insertion point in the table.

2. Under Table Tools on the Ribbon, click the Layout tab and click the Delete button in the Rows & Columns group. A list will appear.

3. Select Delete Table. The table will be deleted from the document.

Practice converting or deleting a table. The instructions below will show you how!

You will need to access practice files in your course online for this lesson. We've placed instructions in the appendix of this book on page 237.

Using Quick Tables

Insert a formatted table quickly by inserting one of Word's built-in Quick Tables.

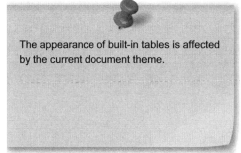

The appearance of built-in tables is affected by the current document theme.

1. Click the Insert tab on the Ribbon and click the Table button in the Tables group. A list of table options will appear.

2. Point to Quick Tables. A gallery of built-in tables will appear. As you point to each built-in table, a description of the table and how it might best be used is shown.

3. Select the table you would like to insert. The table will be inserted in the document. All you have to do is modify the table contents to your needs.

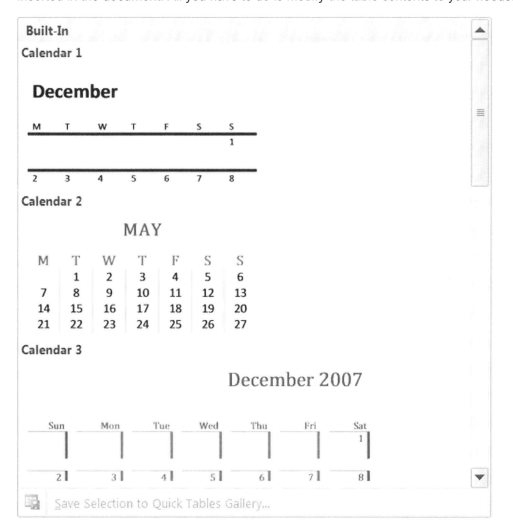

The instructions below will teach you how to use Quick Tables. Be sure to practice.

You will need to access practice files in your course online for this lesson. We've placed instructions in the appendix of this book on page 238.

Answer Key

Microsoft Word Fundamentals

Understanding the Word 2010 Program Screen

I. MATCHING.

1. B. status bar
2. G. Close button
3. E. document window
4. H. Ribbon
5. D. ruler
6. C. insertion point
7. A. File tab
8. F. title bar

Giving Commands in Word – Lesson 2

I. TRUE/FALSE.

1. false
2. true
3. true

Using Command Shortcuts – Lesson 2

I. TRUE/FALSE.

1. false
2. true
3. true

Creating a New Document

I. MULTIPLE CHOICE.

1. Right-click and select New Document.
2. Office.com Templates
3. A new document will automatically appear when you open Word.

Saving a Document – Lesson 2

I. MATCHING.

1. G. Word Macro-Enabled Document
2. H. Web page
3. B. Word XML Document
4. E. Word Document
5. F. plain text
6. A. PDF
7. D. Word 97-2003 Document
8. C. rich text format

Using Help

I. MULTIPLE CHOICE.

1. F1
2. Office Online database
3. all help categories

Document Basics

Selecting and Replacing Text

I. FILL IN THE BLANK.

1. several bits of text
2. the entire document
3. line of text
4. paragraph

Navigating through a Document

I. MATCHING.

1. D. scroll bars
2. C. Home
3. A. Go To command
4. B. navigation keystrokes

Viewing a Document

I. MULTIPLE CHOICE.

1. draft view
2. Select the whole document, then click Ctrl + Z.
3. all the above
4. optimizes the screen for reading, making room for enlarged text and naviational tools

Viewing Multiple Document Windows

I. FILL IN THE BLANK.

1. two
2. synchronous scrolling
3. higher
4. active

Working With and Editing Text

Checking Spelling and Grammar

I. MULTIPLE CHOICE.

1. accepts the spelling or grammar you used and ignores all future occurrences in the document
2. from the location of the insertion point
3. misspellings and grammatical errors
4. green
5. Change

Replacing Text

I. MATCHING.

1. G. searches for wildcards, special characters, or special search operators as added in the "Find what" box
2. F. does not account for punctuation when searching for entered text
3. D. searches for the text in the "Find what" box at the beginning of the word
4. B. searches only for the text that matches the capitalization entered
5. E. allows you to search by and insert special characters
6. H. words that sound the same as the "Find what" text, but are spelled differently
7. A. specifies formatting characteristics you want to find attached to the text in the "Find what" text box
8. C. does not account for spaces or empty paragraph marks

Copying and Moving Text

I. MULTIPLE CHOICE.

1. CTRL + V
2. selects text that will remain in its original location and adds it to the Clipboard
3. all of the above

Formatting Characters and Paragraphs

Review: Fonts

I. MULTIPLE CHOICE.

1. Click the Font button on the Formatting tab and select the desired font.
2. points or pt
3. all of the above
4. CTRL + SHIFT + F
5. select No Color from the Text Highlight Color button

II. TRUE/FALSE.

1. true
2. false
3. true

Creating Lists

I. TRUE/FALSE.

1. true
2. false
3. true

Adding Paragraph Borders and Shading

I. MULTIPLE CHOICE.

1. all of the above
2. Click the Shading tab, then click the Fill list arrow and select the color you want to use.
3. select the No Border option

Setting Tab Stops

I. TRUE/FALSE.
1. true
2. false
3. true
4. false

Using Hanging and First Line Indents

I. MATCHING.
1. A. hanging indent
2. B. first line indent
3. A. hanging indent
4. A. hanging indent
5. B. first line indent

Formatting the Page

Changing Page Orientation and Size

I. MULTIPLE CHOICE.
1. More Paper Sizes
2. 8 1/2 x 11
3. horizontal
4. page orientation

Using Page Breaks

I. MATCHING.
1. A. widow
2. E. page break before
3. C. don't hyphenate
4. D. keep lines together
5. B. orphan
6. F. suppress line numbers

Working with the Page Background

I. FILL IN THE BLANK.
1. page color
2. This section
3. watermark
4. borders
5. Setting

Adding a Cover Page and Page Numbers

I. TRUE/FALSE.
1. true
2. false
3. false
4. true

Working with Themes and Styles

Creating a Style

I. MATCHING.
1. E. character
2. B. table
3. A. linked
4. C. lists
5. D. paragraph

Working with the Styles Gallery

I. TRUE/FALSE.
1. false
2. true
3. false

Comparing and Cleaning Up Styles

I. TRUE/FALSE.
1. true
2. true
3. false

Applying Document Themes

I. FILL IN THE BLANK.
1. Document Themes
2. Theme Fonts
3. customize
4. Theme Effects

Working with Tables

Working with a Table

I. FILL IN THE BLANK.
1. multiple cells
2. SHIFT + TAB
3. left

Working with Cell Formatting

I. TRUE/FALSE.
1. false
2. true
3. false

Inserting and Deleting Rows and Columns

I. TRUE/FALSE.
1. true
2. false
3. false

Working with Sorting and Formulas

I. MULTIPLE CHOICE.

1. equal sign
3. ascending and descending
5. number

2. do not
4. letter

Working with Borders and Shading

I. MULTIPLE CHOICE.

1. They are visible if the table is in the default table format.
3. Shading

2. click the table's move handle

4. select No Border

Using Table Style Options

I. MATCHING.

1. A. First/Last Column
3. B. Banded Rows/Columns

2. C. Header Row
4. D. Total Row

Appendix

Save a new document

1. Click the Save button on the Quick Access Toolbar. The Save As dialog box appears.

2. Type Saved Document.

3. In the Folders List, click Desktop.

4. Click Save.

Save document changes

1. Type your name at the top of the document.

2. Click the Save button on the Quick Access Toolbar.

This is the fastest way to save changes made to a document; you could follow the other method (Click the File tab, select Save) if you prefer.

Insert text

Inserting text is extremely easy, simply click where you want to insert the text and start typing.

1. If necessary, open a new blank document.

2. Type Dear Mr. Nelson,

Delete text

3. Press the Backspace key.

4. Select the word Nelson and press Delete.

5. Type Nielsen, and press Enter.

Select text

1. Open the AcadiaProposal2-2.docx file.

2. Click at the beginning of the word June.

3. Click and hold the left mouse button as you drag the insertion point across the text June Cartwright.

Replace text

Replacing text is easy – once the text you want to replace is selected, simply type the new text.

4. Type your name. The selected text is replaced by your name.

5. Continue to change the address to your details.

Browsing a Document

The Browse Object button provides a quick way to locate specific types of objects in your document.

Browse by object

1. Open the AcadiaProposal2-4.docx file.

2. Click the Select Browse Object button on the vertical scroll bar.

3. Click the Browse by graphic icon .

4. Click the Next Object button until you locate the Filter by Form graphic.

Browse by heading

5. In the same document, switch the Navigation Pane on by clicking the View tab and select the Navigation Pane check box in the Show group.

6. Click the Outlook header.

Browse by page

7. In the Navigation Pane, click the Browse the pages in your document tab.

8. Click page 7.

9. Click the Close button on the Navigation Pane to close it.

Viewing a Document

1. Open the AcadiaProposal2-5.docx file.

2. Click and drag the Zoom slider on the status bar to 200%.

3. Click and drag the Zoom slider on the status bar to 75%.

4. Click the View tab on the Ribbon and click the Two Pages button in the Zoom group.

5. Click the Home tab on the Ribbon and click the Show/Hide button in the Paragraph group to show hidden characters in the document.

6. Click the Show/Hide button again to hide the characters.

Change window size

1. Open the AcadiaProposal2-6.docx file.

2. Play around with the Maximize/Restore Down and Minimize buttons, as well as the resize control.

Split the document window

3. Click the View tab on the Ribbon and click the Split button in the Window group.

4. Click in the middle of the page.

5. Click the Remove Split button on the Ribbon in the Window group.

Switch between document windows

1. Open the AcadiaProposal2-7.docx and AccessArticle.docx files.

2. Click the AcadiaProposal2-7 button on the Windows taskbar.

There is also another way to switch between windows...

3. Click the View tab on the Ribbon and click the Switch Windows button in the Window group. Select the Access Article file.

Arrange document windows

4. Click the Arrange All button on the Ribbon in the Window group. Word arranges the document windows so that you can see both of them at the same time.

Check spelling and grammar in the document

1. Open the CompanyMeeting3-1.docx file.

2. Click the Review tab on the Ribbon and click the Spelling & Grammar button in the Proofing group. The Spelling and Grammar dialog box appears

3. The last name "Willes" is actually a correctly spelled word so click Ignore All.

4. Click Change to capitalize the word "in." Click Change to correct the misspelled word "auxiliary." Select Delete to remove the extra "the."

Once finished with the Spelling and Grammar dialog box, close the document.

5. Click the Close button in the upper-right corner of the dialog box.

Find text

If you're not sure where certain text is located in a document, Word can locate it for you via the Find feature.

1. Open the CompanyMeeting3-2.docx file.

2. Click the Home tab on the Ribbon and click the Find button in the Editing group.

3. Type Explore.

Open the Find and Replace dialog box

4. Click the Find options and additional search commands button and select Advanced Find from the list.

5. Click the Reading Highlight Options button and select Highlight All.

Replacing text

1. Open the CompanyMeeting3-3.docx file.

2. Click the Home tab on the Ribbon and click the Replace button in the Editing group.

3. In the "Find what" text box, type Explore

4. Press Tab and type Travel.

5. Click Replace All and click OK.

Be very careful when using the Replace All command. Remember that Word finds and replaces whole words only.

Word Count

1. Open the CompanyMeeting3-4.docx file.

2. Click the Review tab on the Ribbon and click the Word Count button in the Proofing group.

The Word Count dialog box appears, displaying the number of words, characters, paragraphs, and lines.

3. Click Close.

A quick and easy way to find out how many words are in a document is via the status bar (left-hand side).

Thesaurus

4. Select the word exciting in the first sentence of the memo.

5. Click the Thesaurus button in the Proofing group. The Research task pane appears.

6. Point to the word thrilling, click its list arrow, and select Insert.

Insert symbols

1. Open the CompanyMeeting3-5.docx file.

2. Position the insertion point after the first occurrence of the text Travel Canada.

3. Click the Insert tab on the Ribbon and click the Symbol button in the Symbols group.

The Symbol dialog box appears.

4. Click the Copyright symbol.

5. Repeat these steps to insert a copyright symbol after the second occurrence of the text Travel Canada.

Insert an equation

If you are working in Compatibility mode, existing equations are inserted as pictures and can't be edited.

6. Position the insertion point at the end of the TO: All Staff line.

7. Click the Equation button in the Symbols group on the Ribbon.

A placeholder for the equation appears in the document and the Equation Tools appear on the Ribbon. Note the Design tab that appears on the Ribbon under Equation Tools, and the variety of different commands that are available on this tab.

If necessary, use the Zoom control to magnify the equation so you can see it better.

8. Click the Undo button on the Quick Access Toolbar.

Cut text

When you *cut* text, it is removed from its original location and placed in a temporary storage area called the Clipboard.

1. Open the Meeting Schedule1.docx file.

2. Select the four lines of the schedule.

3. Click the Home tab on the Ribbon and click the Cut button in the Clipboard group.

The selected text is cut, or removed, from the document and placed on the Office Clipboard (more on the Clipboard in the next lesson).

Paste text

After cutting or copying text you can then *paste* it in a new location.

4. Open the CompanyMeeting3-6.docx file.

5. Click below the text "The schedule for the meeting is as follows" and click the Paste button in the Clipboard group on the Ribbon.

The cut text is pasted onto the document.

Repeat the process by cutting the text "An overhead display will be available" in the Meeting Schedule1.docx file and pasting it after the schedule in the CompanyMeeting3-6.docx file.

Use paste options

1. Open the CompanyMeeting3-7.docx file.

2. Select the word Thursday in the document, right-click and select Cut.

3. Move your mouse to the end of the 3rd line RE: Company Meeting and select Paste on the home tab.

4. Click the Paste Options button that appears and click Merge Formatting.

Collecting Multiple Items to Move or Copy

1. Open the CompanyMeeting3-8.docx and MeetingSchedule2.docx files.

2. In the MeetingSchedule2.docx file, click the Home tab and click the Dialog Box Launcher in the Clipboard group.

3. Select the first item in the bulleted list (Breakfast, 8:00) and copy.

4. Select the last items in the bulleted list (Luncheon, 12:00) and copy.

5. Go to the CompanyMeeting3-8.docx file, click the Home tab and click the Dialog Box Launcher in the Clipboard group.

6. Insert your mouse at the beginning of the schedule and click the Breakfast line item in the Clipboard to paste it.

7. Insert your mouse at the end of the schedule and click the Luncheon line item in the Clipboard to paste it.

Using Undo, Redo and Repeat

1. Open the Company Meeting3-9.docx file.

2. Delete the text TO: All Staff.

3. Delete the first paragraph of the letter.

Undo multiple actions

4. Click the Undo button list arrow on the Quick Access Toolbar.

5. Point to the second Typing action in the list. Two actions should now be selected.

6. Click the left mouse button.

Both deleted items reappear.

Changing Font Type

1. Open the DirectorsMeeting4-1.docx file.

2. Select the text Board of Directors Meeting.

3. Click the Home tab on the Ribbon and click the Font list arrow in the Font group.

4. Select Cambria from the list.

Changing Font Size

1. Open the DirectorsMeeting4-2.docx file.

2. Select the text Board of Directors Meeting.

3. Click the Home tab on the Ribbon and click the Font Size list arrow in the Font group.

4. Select 18 pt from the list.

Changing Font Color and Highlighting Text

Using color in your documents helps certain text stand out from the rest.

Change font color

1. Open the DirectorsMeeting4-3.docx file.

2. Select the text Board of Directors Meeting.

3. Click the Home tab on the Ribbon and click the Font Color button list arrow in the Font group.

4. Select a blue color.

To view more color options, click the Font Color button list arrow and select More Colors.

Highlight text

5. Select the text Acadia received only one customer complaint because of a delay.

6. Click the Home tab on the Ribbon and click the Text Highlight Color button in the Font group.

Changing Font Styles

1. Open the DirectorsMeeting4-4.docx file.

2. Select the text New Communications Director.

3. Click the Bold icon in the Font group on the Home tab.

4. Select the 5th last line (Department Contracts Change % Change)

5. Click the Bold icon and the Italics icon in the Font group on the Home tab.

Applying Spacing and Ligatures

Note that ligatures can only be applied to OpenType fonts such as those in Word 2010. If you are working in Compatibility mode, Ligatures and any other OpenType Features will not be available.

Apply Ligatures

1. Open the Board of Directors Meeting4-5.docx file.

2. Select the text New Communications Director.

3. Click the Dialog Box Launcher in the Font group on the Home tab.

4. Click the Advanced tab.

5. Select Standard and Contextual from the Ligatures list arrow.

Note: if this option is not available, first save the document as a Word 2010 file.

6. Click OK.

Create bulleted and numbered lists

1. Open the DirectorsMeeting4-6.docx file.

2. Select the four lines below the first paragraph, beginning with Written formal client correspondence and ending with Updating Acadia's web site.

3. Click the Home tab on the Ribbon and click the Bullets button in the Paragraph group.

Create a multilevel list

4. Click the Multilevel List button in the Paragraph group.

5. We don't want to create a multilevel list right now, so click anywhere outside the list to close it.

Changing Paragraph Alignment

1. Open the DirectorsMeeting4-7.docx file.

2. Select the Board of Directors Meeting heading.

3. Click the Home tab on the Ribbon and select the Center button in the Paragraph group.

The heading is centered on the page.

Add a paragraph border

1. Open the DirectorsMeeting4-8.docx file.

2. Position the insertion point anywhere inside the New Communications Director heading.

3. On the Home tab on the Ribbon, click the Border button list arrow in the Paragraph group.

4. Select Borders and Shading from the list.

5. Select the Borders tab.

6. Click the Color list arrow and select a shade of blue.

7. Click the bottom border button and click OK.

Word applies a border below the selected paragraph.

Changing Line Spacing

1. Open the DirectorsMeeting4-9.docx file.

2. Select all of the text in the document below the New Communications Director heading.

3. On the Home tab on the Ribbon, click the Line Spacing button in the Paragraph group.

4. Select 1.5 from the list.

Changing Spacing Between Paragraphs

1. Open the DirectorsMeeting4-10.docx file.

2. Position the insertion point anywhere inside the New Communications Director heading.

3. On the Home tab on the Ribbon, click the Dialog Box Launcher in the Paragraph group.

4. Under Spacing, use the up and down arrow buttons to apply 6 pt spacing before and 12 pt spacing after the paragraph.

5. Click OK.

Using the Format Painter

1. Open the DirectorsMeeting4-11.docx file.

2. Select the New Communications Director heading.

3. On the Home tab on the Ribbon, click the Format Painter button in the Clipboard group.

To apply copied formatting more than once you would double-click the Format Painter button instead of single-clicking.

4. Click and drag the insertion point across the The Month in Review heading.

The copied formatting is applied to the selected text and the Format Painter tool is deactivated.

Setting Tab Stops

Word has left tab stops set at every half-inch by default.

Set tabs with the ruler

In order to set tabs using the ruler, the ruler must be displayed.

1. Open the DirectorsMeeting4-12.docx file.

2. Select the last five lines of the document.

We want to apply a left tab stop to the selected paragraphs. The Left Tab indicator is already displayed in the Tab alignment box, so go ahead and move on to the next step.

3. Click the 1" mark on the ruler.

Let's insert another tab stop using the ruler.

4. With the same text still selected, click the Tab selector box on the ruler until the Center Tab indicator appears.

5. Click the 3" mark on the ruler.

Set tabs with the Tabs dialog box

6. If necessary, click the Home tab on the Ribbon.

7. Click the Dialog Box Launcher in the Paragraph group.

8. Click the Tabs button near the bottom of the dialog box.

9. Type 4.5 in the Tab stop position box, click the Right option under Alignment, and click Set.

Now let's insert a decimal tab stop with a dotted leader.

10. Type 5.5 in the Tab stop position box, click the Decimal option under Alignment, click 2 under Leader, and click Set.

11. Click OK to apply the tab settings to the selected text.

Adjust a tab stop with the ruler

1. Open the DirectorsMeeting4-13.docx file.

2. Select the last 5 lines in the document.

3. In the ruler at the top, drag that Decimal tab stop to 6".

Adjust a tab stop with the Tabs dialog box

4. With the selection still active, click the Dialog Box Launcher in the Paragraph group on the Home tab.

5. Click the Tabs button.

6. Select the 6" tab stop in the Tab stop position list.

7. Click the Clear button.

Adjust a tab leader

8. With the Tab dialog box still open, select the 4.5" tab stop in the Tab stop position list.

9. Select the 2......... Leader.

10. Click Set.

11. Click OK.

Left indent

1. Open the DirectorsMeeting4-14.docx file.

2. Position the insertion point anywhere inside the paragraph below the New Communications Director heading.

3. On the Home tab on the Ribbon, click the Increase Indent button in the Paragraph group.

The paragraph is indented .25".

Another way to indent a paragraph

4. Position the insertion point anywhere inside the paragraph below the Month in Review heading.

5. On the Home tab on the Ribbon, click the Dialog Box Launcher in the Paragraph group.

6. Type .25 in the Left box under Indentation. Click OK when you're finished.

Right indent

7. Click and drag the Right indent marker on the ruler to the 6" mark.

Hanging indent

1. Open the DirectorsMeeting4-15.docx file.

2. Position the insertion point anywhere inside the paragraph below the New Communications Director heading.

3. On the Home tab on the Ribbon, click the Dialog Box Launcher in the Paragraph group.

4. Click the Special list arrow under Indentation and select Hanging from the list.

5. Type .5 in the By box and click OK.

First line indent

6. Position the insertion point anywhere inside the paragraph below the Month in Review heading.

7. Click and drag the First Line indent marker to the 1" mark on the ruler.

Adjusting Margins

1. Open the FormatPage5-1.docx file.

2. Click the Page Layout tab on the Ribbon and click the Margins button in the Page Setup group.

A list of popular margin settings appears.

3. Select Narrow from the list.

The document's margins are adjusted.

Page orientation

Portrait orientation is the default page orientation in Word.

1. Open the FormatPage5-2.docx file and navigate to Page 2.

2. Click the Page Layout tab on the Ribbon and click the Orientation button in the Page Setup group.

3. Select Landscape.

Page size

Consider your printer's printing capabilities before you decide on a paper size.

4. On the Page Layout tab on the Ribbon, click the Size button in the Page Setup group.

5. Select More Paper Sizes from the list.

6. Type 11 in the Height box and click OK.

7. Type 17 in the Width box and click OK.

Using Columns

It may be easiest to work through this lesson with the Show Characters feature turned on. To do this, click the Home tab on the Ribbon and click the Show/Hide button in the Paragraph group.

Format columns

Newsletters and magazine articles are often arranged in two or more columns.

1. Open the FormatPage5-3.docx file.

2. Navigate to Page 2 and click anywhere in the first paragraph.

3. Click the Page Layout tab on the Ribbon and click the Columns button in the Page Setup group.

A list of popular column layouts appears. If the column layout you want to use doesn't appear in this list, click More Columns to open the Columns dialog box and specify the appropriate options.

4. Select Two from the list.

Word arranges the text on the page into two columns.

If you want to adjust a column layout after it has been applied, click the Columns button in the Page Setup group and select More Columns from the list.

Use a column break

If you wanted to leave a column empty halfway down the page to leave space for a pull quote or picture, you would need to insert a column break. Inserting a column break allows you to continue your text in the next column.

5. Position the insertion point at the beginning of the Filter by Selection heading (near the bottom of the first column).

6. Click the Breaks button in the Page Setup group and select Column from the list.

The column break is inserted and the insertion point jumps to the beginning of the next column.

Start a new page

One thing to remember is using a page break instead of pressing the ENTER key a bunch of times prevents many formatting issues from occurring later in the document.

1. Open the FormatPage5-4.docx file.

2. Navigate to Page 5 and position the insertion point at the beginning of the PowerPoint heading.

3. Click the Insert tab on the Ribbon and click the Page Break button in the Pages group.

Word inserts a page break at the insertion point.

Use paragraph line and page breaks

4. Navigate to the bottom of Page 6 and position the insertion point anywhere in the Creating a rule using the Rules Wizard heading.

5. Click the Page Layout tab on the Ribbon and click the Dialog Box Launcher in the Paragraph group.

The Indents and Spacing tab of the Paragraph dialog box appears. If you have used the Line and Page Breaks tab recently however, it may appear instead.

6. Click the Line and Page Breaks tab and select Keep with next under Pagination. Click OK when you're finished.

The selected heading jumps to the next page, thus "keeping it with next".

Working with Section Breaks

1. Open the FormatPage5-5.docx file.

2. Navigate to Page 7 and position the insertion point at the end of the paragraph before the Managing rules section.

3. Click the Page Layout tab on the Ribbon and click the Breaks button in the Page Setup group.

A list of break types appears.

4. Under Section Breaks, select Next Page.

A Next Page section break is inserted into the document.

Working with Line Numbers

Line numbers are extremely useful when you need to refer to a specific line in a document, such as a script or a legal contract.

1. Open the FormatPage5-6.docx file.

2. Navigate to Page 3.

3. Click the Page Layout tab on the Ribbon and click the Line Numbers button in the Page Setup group.

4. Select Restart Each Page from the list.

Line numbers appear next to every line on the page.

Working with Hyphenation

Hyphenation is turned OFF by default.

1. Open the FormatPage5-7.docx file.

2. Click the Page Layout tab on the Ribbon and click the Hyphenation button in the Page Setup group.

3. Select Automatic.

Add page borders

1. Open the FormatPage5-8.docx file.

2. Navigate to Page 8.

3. Click the Page Layout tab on the Ribbon and click the Page Borders button in the Page Background group.

The Page Border tab of the Borders and Shading dialog box appears.

4. Click the Color list arrow and select a blue color.

5. Click the top, bottom, left and right edge of the diagram in the Preview section.

6. Click the Apply to list arrow and select This section from the list.

7. Click OK.

The borders are applied to the section.

Add page color

8. Click the Page Layout tab on the Ribbon and click the Page Color button in the Page Background group.

9. Select Light Green.

Add a watermark

10. Click the Page Layout tab on the Ribbon and click the Watermark button in the Page Background group.

11. Select Draft 1 from the Disclaimers section.

12. Click OK.

Cover page

You don't need to position the insertion point on the first page of the document in order to insert a cover page, Word will insert the cover page at the beginning of the document no matter where the insertion point is located.

1. Open the FormatPage5-9.docx file.

2. Click the Insert tab on the Ribbon and click the Cover Page button in the Pages group.

A list of built-in cover pages appears. Each design has a name, making it easier to match up with other built-in elements that have been applied to the document.

3. Select the Motion cover page.

The selected cover page is inserted at the beginning of the document.

Page numbers

Word 2010 makes inserting page numbers easier than ever.

4. Click the Page Number button in the Header & Footer group on the Ribbon.

A list of locations appears.

5. Point to Top of Page.

A list of page number styles appears.

6. Select the Accent Bar 1 style.

Page numbers now appear on all pages in the document.

To modify how a page number is formatted, click the Insert tab on the Ribbon, click the Page Number button in the Header & Footer group, and select Format Page Numbers.

Insert a built-in header or footer

1. Open the FormatPage5-10.docx file.

2. Click the Insert tab on the Ribbon and click the Footer button in the Header & Footer group.

3. Select Edit Footer from the list. The Design tab appears on the Ribbon under Header & Footer Tools.

4. Click the Different Odd & Even Pages check box in the Options group.

5. Click the Close Header & Footer button in the Close group.

6. Go to Page 1, click the Insert tab on the Ribbon and click the Footer button in the Header & Footer group.

A list of footer options appears. To insert a built-in footer, simply select an option from this list. Select an odd-page footer.

Now go to Page 2 and insert an even-page footer.

Applying a Style

1. Open the Management6-1.docx file.

2. Select the text Annual Management Meeting.

3. Click the Home tab on the Ribbon and select the Title style from the Styles Gallery in the Styles group.

Depending on the size of your program window, you may have to click the More button in the Styles group in order to access the Title style.

4. Select the text Seminar Schedule and apply the Subtitle style to it.

Apply a different Quick Style set

5. Click the Change Styles button in the Styles group.

6. Point to Style Set and select Formal from the list.

Creating a Style

1. Open the Management6-2.docx file.

2. Apply Bold formatting to the text "The Internet and Travel," and change its font size to 14 pt.

3. With the text The Internet and Travel still selected, right-click the text, select Styles and then click Save Selection as a New Quick Style from the contextual menu.

4. Type Seminar in the Name text box.

5. Click OK.

Modify a style

1. Open the Management6-3.docx file.

2. Select the text The Internet and Travel.

3. Change the font size to 11pt by selecting 11 from the Font Size list in the Font group on the Home tab.

4. With the text still selected, right-click the Seminar style in the Styles Gallery on the Home tab and select Update Seminar to Match Selection.

Delete a style

5. Click the Dialog Box Launcher in the Styles Group.

6. Click the list arrow to the right of the Seminar style and select Delete Seminar.

7. Click Yes.

Add a style to the Styles Gallery

1. Open the Management6-4.docx file.

2. Click the Home tab on the Ribbon and click the Dialog Box Launcher in the Styles group.

3. Click the Options link.

4. Click the Select styles to show list arrow and select All styles. Click OK.

5. Point to the Salutation style, click its list arrow, and select Add to Quick Style Gallery from the list.

Remove a style from the Styles Gallery

6. Right-click the Salutation style in the Styles Gallery.

7. Select Remove from Quick Style Gallery from the contextual menu.

Creating a New Quick Style Set

1. Open the Management6-5.docx file.

2. Click the Home tab on the Ribbon. If you didn't do so in the "Working with the Styles Gallery" lesson, add/remove styles in the Styles Gallery so that only those you want to include in the new style set appear in the Gallery.

3. Click the Change Styles button in the Styles group.

4. Point to Style Set and select Save as Quick Style Set from the menu.

5. Click inside the File name text box and type Management.

You could change this name so that it makes more sense to your users, for example you could name the style set "Popular" so that your users know it contains their most commonly-used commands.

6. Click Save.

Selecting, Removing, and Printing Styles

1. Open the Management6-6.docx file.

2. Select The Internet and Travel and Better Team Communication.

3. Click the Home tab on the Ribbon and select the Strong style from the Styles Gallery in the Styles group.

Select text that uses the same style

4. Click the Home tab on the Ribbon and right-click the Strong style in the Styles gallery in the Styles group.

5. Click Select All Instances from the list.

Remove a style from text

6. Click the Home tab on the Ribbon and click the Dialog Box Launcher in the Styles group.

7. Click the Strong list arrow and select Clear Formatting of All Instance(s).

Print styles

8. Click the File tab and select Print.

9. Click the Print all pages list arrow and select Styles.

10. Click Print.

Clean up styles

1. Open the Management6-7.docx file.

2. Apply the Intense Reference style to the Exploring Childcare line.

3. Click the Home tab on the Ribbon and click the Dialog Box Launcher in the Styles group.

4. Click the Style Inspector button in the Styles task pane.

5. Select the text Better Team Communication.

Compare formatted text to other formatted text

6. Click the Reveal Formatting button.

7. Click the Compare to another selection check box in the Reveal Formatting task pane.

8. Select the text Exploring Childcare.

9. Close the Reveal Formatting task pane, the Style Inspector, and the Styles task pane by clicking their Close buttons.

Applying Document Themes

It is important to note that document themes will not show up properly if the document is opened in an earlier version of Word. Keep this in mind when sending documents out to colleagues, clients, etc. who may not have Word 2010 installed.

Apply a document theme

1. Open the Management6-8.docx file.

2. Click the Page Layout tab on the Ribbon and click the Themes button in the Themes group.

3. Select the Opulent theme.

Customize a document theme

4. Click the Theme Fonts button in the Themes group and select the Metro font from the list.

Creating New Theme Colors and Fonts

1. Open the Management6-9.docx file.

2. Click the Page Layout tab on the Ribbon and click the Theme Colors button in the Themes group.

3. Select Create New Theme Colors from the list.

4. Specify that several of your favorite colors be included in the Color Theme.

5. Click in the Name box and type Acadia.

6. Click Save.

Save a New Document Theme

1. Open the Management6-10.docx file.

2. Apply the Acadia theme color to the document.

3. Apply the Foundry theme font to the document.

4. Click the Page Layout tab on the Ribbon and click the Themes button in the Themes group.

5. Select Save Current Theme.

6. Type Acadia and click Save.

Open up the Themes Gallery and your new Acadia theme will be there.

Insert a table

1. Open a new Word document.

2. Click the Insert tab on the Ribbon and click the Table button in the Tables group.

3. In the grid, select a section that is three columns wide by four rows tall.

Move between cells

1. Open the SalesReps9-1.docx file.

2. Click the first cell in the table.

3. Type Last.

4. Click the first cell in the second column and type First. Click the first cell in the third column and type Sales.

5. Enter the following text in the table:

Jones   Marvin   1200
McKenzie   Shandra   1400

Just like other elements in Word, you have to select the parts of a table in order to work with them.

6. If it's not already there, position the insertion point anywhere in the third row of the table.

7. Under Table Tools on the Ribbon, click the Layout tab and click the Select button in the Table group.

8. Select Row from the list.

9. Click anywhere outside the table to deselect the cells.

10. Select the Marvin and Shandra cells.

Resize a table

1. Open the SalesReps9-2.docx file and make sure you are in Print Layout view. You can do this by checking the status bar (the Print Layout button should be highlighted orange) or by clicking the View tab and checking out the Document Views group.

2. Click anywhere inside the table to activate it.

3. Click and drag the table's resize handle to the left, until the table is about five inches wide by one inch tall.

Move a table

4. Click and drag the table's move handle down about an inch.

Adjusting Table Alignment and Text Wrapping

This lesson is very important, because it shows you how to specify how the text on a page interacts with a table. For example, do you want text to wrap around the entire table, or the left side of the table only?

1. Open the SalesReps9-3.docx file.

2. Click anywhere inside the table and then click the table's move handle to select the entire table.

3. Under Table Tools on the Ribbon, click the Layout tab and click the Properties button in the Table group.

4. Click the Center option and click OK.

You can also use the Table Properties dialog box to adjust rows, columns and cells.

Working with Cell Formatting

You can also work with cell formatting to customize how data appears inside a table. For example, you can align text horizontally and vertically in a cell, change text direction, and adjust cell margins.

Align cell contents

1. Open the SalesReps9-4.docx file.

2. Select the first row in the table.

3. Under Table Tools on the Ribbon, click the Layout tab and click the Align Bottom Center button in the Alignment group.

Change text direction

4. With the top row still selected, click the Text Direction button in the Alignment group.

5. Click the Text Direction button again.

6. Click the Undo button on the Quick Access Toolbar twice.

Change cell margins

7. Click anywhere inside the table.

8. Click the Cell Margins button in the Alignment group.

9. Type .05 in the Top text box.

10. Click the Allow spacing between cells check box and type .03 in the text box.

11. Click OK.

Reset the margins to their original settings

1. Click anywhere inside the table.

2. Under Table Tools on the Ribbon, click the Layout tab and click the Cell Margins button in the Alignment group.

3. Type 0.

4. Type 0 in the Allow spacing between cells text box, and then click the Allow spacing between cells check box to deselect it.

5. Click OK.

Merge cells

1. Open the SalesReps9-6.docx file.

2. Select the bottom row of the table.

3. Under Table Tools on the Ribbon, click the Layout tab and click the Merge Cells button in the Merge group.

Split a cell

4. With the bottom row still selected, click the Split Cells button in the Merge group.

5. Type 3 in the Number of columns text box and click OK.

6. Select the third row in the table.

7. Click the Split Table button in the Merge group.

8. The new table may be on top of the first. Select one of the tables and move it to see the other. Click anywhere in the second table to activate it, then click and drag the table's move handle downward about an inch.

9. Click the Undo button on the Quick Access Toolbar twice.

Inserting and Deleting Rows and Columns

Insert a row

1. Open the SalesReps9-7.docx file.

2. Select the first row in the table.

3. Under Table Tools on the Ribbon, click the Layout tab and click the Insert Below button in the Rows & Columns group.

Delete a row or column

4. Click the Delete button in the Rows & Columns group.

5. Select Delete Rows from the list.

Adjust column width

1. Open the SalesReps9-8.docx file.

2. Select the third column in the table.

3. Click the Layout tab, then the Width text box in the Cell Size group and type 1.

Draw borders

1. Open the SalesReps9-9.docx file.

2. Under Table Tools on the Ribbon, click the Design tab and click the Draw Table button in the Draw Borders group.

3. Draw a line down the middle of the last cell of the first column.

Erase borders

4. Click the Eraser button on the Ribbon in the Draw Borders group.

5. Click and drag the eraser across the border you just inserted.

6. In the fourth row, erase the border that separates the first and second cells.

Sort table data

The Sort feature can come in extremely handy – especially if you have large amounts of data.

1. Open the SalesReps9-10.docx file.

2. Select the first three rows in the table.

3. Under Table Tools on the Ribbon, click the Layout tab and click the Sort button in the Data group.

Depending on the size of your program window, you may need to click the Table Data button in the Data group and then click the Sort button.

4. Click the Sort by list arrow and select Sales from the list.

5. Click the Descending option under Sort by, and click OK.

Use formulas in a table

6. Position the insertion point in the last cell of the third column.

7. Under Table Tools on the Ribbon, click the Layout tab and click the Formula button in the Data group.

The Formula dialog box appears.

8. Type =SUM(ABOVE) in the Formula text box.

Remember: All formulas start with an equal sign (=), followed by a function name (such as SUM), followed by parentheses containing the location of the cells on which you want to perform the calculation.

Use the Number format list arrow to define how the formula result appears. Use the Paste function list arrow to build a formula using built-in functions.

9. Click OK.

It's important to note that formulas don't recalculate automatically in Word like they do in Excel. This is an important fact to remember if you or your students are used to using Excel.

Apply a Table Border

1. Open the SalesReps9-11.docx file.

2. Select the entire table.

3. Under Table Tools on the Ribbon, click the Design tab and click the Borders list arrow in the Table Styles group.

4. Select No Border.

View gridlines

Gridlines are dashed lines that show you the location of the table cell borders. They do not appear by default.

5. Under Table Tools on the Ribbon, click the Layout tab and click the View Gridlines button in the Table group.

Apply a fill color

6. Select the first row of the table.

7. Under Table Tools on the Ribbon, click the Design tab, and click the Shading list arrow in the Table Styles group.

8. Select a Light Blue color.

The first row now has a light blue fill color.

9. Select the entire table.

10. Under Table Tools on the Ribbon, click the Design tab and click the Borders list arrow in the Table Styles group.

11. Select All Borders.

Apply a table style

1. Open the SalesReps9-12.docx file.

2. Select the table.

3. Under Table Tools on the Ribbon, click the Design tab.

4. Click the More button in the Table Styles group, and select the Medium Shading 1 – Accent 1 table style.

Create a custom table style

5. With the table still selected, click the More button in the Table Styles group.

6. Select New Table Style. The Create New Style from Formatting dialog box appears.

You can make the new table style available only in the current document or for new documents as well. Select either the Only in this document or the New documents based on this template option in the dialog box.

7. Click Cancel to close the dialog box.

Using Table Style Options

1. Open the SalesReps9-13.docx file.

2. Select the table.

3. Under Table Tools on the Ribbon, click the Design tab.

4. Select the Total Row option in the Table Style Options group.

The last row in the table, the Total row, is formatted.

Convert a table to text

1. Open the SalesReps9-14.docx file.

2. Click anywhere inside the table.

3. Under Table Tools on the Ribbon, click the Layout tab and click the Convert to Text button in the Data group.

4. Select Tabs.

5. Click OK.

Delete a table

6. Click the Undo button on the Quick Access Toolbar to undo the table conversion.

7. Click anywhere inside the table.

8. Under Table Tools on the Ribbon, click the Layout tab and click the Delete button in the Rows & Columns group.

9. Select Delete Table from the list.

Using Quick Tables

Just like you can use document templates to create special types of documents, you can use Quick Tables to create special types of tables.

1. Open a new document.

2. Click the Insert tab on the Ribbon and click the Table button in the Tables group.

3. Point to Quick Tables.

4. Select the Calendar 2 option.

You can modify a Quick Table's appearance just like you would any other table.